SUSTAINABLE URBAN LANDSCAPES

The Surrey Design Charrette

SUSTAINABLE URBAN LANDSCAPES

THE SURREY DESIGN CHARRETTE

A Project of the
University of British Columbia
James Taylor Chair in Landscape
and Liveable Environments

Edited by Patrick M. Condon
Foreword by Doug Kelbaugh
Essay by William R. Morrish

Major Funding from:

Additional funding from:

THE REAL ESTATE
FOUNDATION
OF BRITISH COLUMBIA

SURREY
CITY OF PARKS

Published by the University of British Columbia
    James Taylor Chair in Landscape and Liveable Environments
Designed by Kenneth Hughes
Production assistance by Elizabeth Watts and Alison Arsenault
Copy edited by Joanne Richardson
Typesetting by Iris Schindel
Printed and bound by Friesen's Press, Manitoba, Canada
Distributed by the University of British Columbia Press
    6344 Memorial Road
    University of British Columbia
    Vancouver, British Columbia
    Canada V6T 1Z2

Based on work presented at a design charrette held in September of 1995 at the University of British Columbia

Canadian Cataloguing in Publication Data

Main entry under title:

Sustainable urban landscapes

    Includes bibliographical references.
    ISBN 0-88865-535-5

1. City planning – Environmental aspects – British Columbia – Surrey. 2. Planned unit developments – British Columbia – Surrey. 3. City planning – British Columbia.
4. Sustainable development – British Columbia. I. Condon, Patrick M.
II. University of British Columbia. James Taylor Chair in Landscape and Liveable Environments.

HT169.C32S92 1996   711'.4'0971133   C96-910263-1

ACKNOWLEDGEMENTS

Many organizations and individuals cooperated to make this charrette a reality. Their efforts were motivated by a shared belief—the belief that the careful design of individual sites is a crucial ingredient for a more sustainable urban region. We owe our greatest expression of thanks to the anonymous donor to the James Taylor Chair in Landscapes and Liveable Environments. Without this support there would be no chair, no charrette, and no publication.

For this first charrette project we owe a special acknowledgment to the Real Estate Foundation of British Columbia for providing major project funding. Much of their support was used to finance this publication. We also thank the City of Surrey for offering the case study site, for providing a wealth of background material, for their financial support for the project, and for hosting the briefing session and the public presentation in Surrey. Our special thanks to Mayor Robert Bose, who enthusiastically embraced the objectives of our project, and to Mr. Burton Leon, Manager of Policy and Long Range Planning, for committing so much of his time and the time of his colleagues to this project.

We are also indebted for the strong support shown by the Province of British Columbia, Ministry of Municipal Affairs, Hon. Darlene Marzari, Minister, and Joan Sawicki, MLA, Parliamentary Secretary and to Erik Karlsen, Director of Special Projects for his early and continuing support.

Also crucial was the direction provided by the members of our advisory board: Mr. Michael Geller, Dr. Penelope Gurstein, Professor Sanford Hirshen, Mr. Burton Leon, Mr. Erik Karlsen, Mr. Hugh Kellas, Mr. Dale McClanaghan, Ms. Stacy Moriarty, Professor Patrick Mooney, Mr. Kelvin Neufeld, Dr. John Robinson, and Ms. Elizabeth Watts. Elizabeth Watts performed a second vital role in her capacity as Charrette Coordinator.

In the "last but not least" category are the team leaders and students who actually produced all of the drawings contained in this book. A listing of the team leaders, with short biographies, can be found in the appendix. They are living proof that you can be over forty and still stay up all night working to deadline. The pictures of all of the student participants (except for those who somehow slipped out when the shutter was snapped) and their names are featured at the beginning of each design section. Again, many thanks to these students for bringing fresh ideas to the project and for challenging the team leaders to reach for the best and most sustainable solutions possible.

Doug Kelbaugh, FAIA, Professor of Architecture & Urban Design at the University of Washington not only participated in the charrette and provided the Foreword for this publication, he was also our advisor during the planning and design–programming phase. Thank you Professor Kelbaugh for all of your helpful ideas.

Finally, a special thanks to the Design Center for the American Urban Landscape at the University of Minnesota. We thank the Design Center, and Catherine Brown and William Morrish in particular, for bringing the words *design*, *urban*, and *landscape* together. Due to their efforts, not only are the words coming together, but so, it seems, is the practice of urban landscape design.

FOREWORD

What is a design charrette? The short answer is that it is an illustrated brainstorm. A longer answer emerged for the University of British Columbia (UBC) last September, when its Landscape Architecture Program hosted a five-day intensive workshop. Four competing teams of students, led by design professionals, developed different design solutions for a new town site in Surrey, where they presented them at a well-attended public review. Distinguished team leaders, representing the disciplines of architecture and landscape architecture, were recruited both locally and from all over the continent. A charrette typically deals with an urban design issue of social and civic importance. It is meant to provide community clienteles with feasible but creative solutions to pressing issues, as opposed to providing faculty and students with a theoretical or pedagogic exercise. There are three basic types of charrettes: (1) those that test new public policies or design ideas on real sites, (2) those that respond to requests for help from neighbourhood groups or government agencies, and (3) those that initiate unsolicited proposals for a glaring problem or opportunity presented by a specific site. Some charrettes are hybrids, such as those that test a new idea on a site that is under-utilized. The UBC charrette combined all three types in that it tested government policies on an under-developed site at the request of the City of Surrey. This alone is an ambitious and significant undertaking.

Why hold a charrette? The answer is that, in their formative stages, the planning efforts for a region need the benefit of creative physical design. Neighbourhoods, towns, cities, and regions should not be planned, or even zoned, according to abstract policies and non-visual formulae drafted by lawyers, lawmakers, and bureaucrats who have not enlisted the help of design professionals. Such methods have led to zoning codes as thick as telephone books and as difficult to decipher as tax regulations. Often these land-use and zoning codes prohibit – sometimes on purpose, sometimes inadvertently – making a traditional town or neighbourhood. To build anything resembling a "High Street" or "Elm Street" in many North American municipalities is now actually against the law! Designing a region, like designing a building, should not be done *ex novo*; it is an interactive process that needs to illustrate and to test proposed policies and laws in three dimensions before adopting them. It is not only a question of designers and planners validating policy and laws; it is also very much a question of design informing policy. Design is more than a service to be bought by the pound or by the hour and plugged in at the end of a problem-solving process. It is too powerfully integrative and formulative to be withheld until policy and program are in place. Design charrettes can brainstorm a problem in a way that liberates latent and inevitable possibilities. It can reveal what a project's site and program want to be as well as illustrate what special interest groups and stakeholders desire. Because the design charrette looks at a problem holistically, the results are not likely to fall prey to specialized thinking and political tinkering. Charrettes kill many birds with one stone: they help the community solve problems and build consensus; they test new ideas and policies that are generated within the community, the design professions, or the university; they seize on forgotten places and nascent possibilities; they build according to how the community understands itself; they bring to town and to campus leading designers that would otherwise be unaffordable; and they stimulate and bring together faculty and students while putting to good use university resources and expertise. To boot, they do all these things economically. By sponsoring this event, the UBC Landscape Architecture Program has made good use of its financial resources and its intellectual capital.

Having organized and participated in over a dozen charrettes, I can attest that this charrette was both very well organized and productive. The participants were sent a well-conceived and well-written programme, with background information, in advance of the event. All the key parties – an impressive array of citizens and officials – were in Surrey for the initial briefing before touring the site by bus. Large multi-disciplinary teams worked and shared food under the same roof for five days. Each team was equipped with the expertise, the tools, and the judgment to make the long chain of decisions that constitutes design. To my knowledge, there were more team leaders involved in this than in any previous charrette – four highly qualified design professionals on each team. That is a lot of design horsepower. Like all charrette deadlines, the Friday public presentation ensured that decisions would not be postponed, as they tend to be in normal work schedules while awaiting input from other parties. The teams accomplished a remarkable amount of work in a remarkably short period. Like all charrettes, it was short-lived and sometimes subject to wrong turns or the truncated kind of thinking which is forced upon one by a clock that ticks much faster than normal. Fortunately, all the teams came up with strong ideas around which to coalesce their designs. The results, as always, were at the same time refreshingly unpredictable and comfortably assuring. The chemistry of both collaboration among teammates and friendly competition between teams unleashed ideas that would have possibly been overlooked in slower-paced, more linear approaches to design. Like all charrettes, the collective energy – at times rife with confusion – gave rise to fertile creativity. Adrenaline always generates bad ideas as well as good ones, and the results of this compressed and febrile creativity must now be widely and carefully reviewed. The charrette process, by its very nature, tends to encourage a no-holds-barred approach to design. Because design teams focus on a single place and want to make sure all the cards are played, they are sometimes loath to leave out any promising or imaginative ideas. Consequently, designs sometimes become too elaborate and optimistic. On the other hand, a charrette represents a given site's moment in the spotlight and should not be overly shackled by normal budgetary and legal constraints. In any case, many ideas must now be edited by the many different constituencies, and those that survive then need to be reworked and refined. This book is an invitation to join that ongoing process.

For Patrick Condon and the other organizers and participants, what underlies this book is a deeper worry: a fundamental dissatisfaction with and alarm over the direction that metropolitan development has taken in recent decades. This is equally true in my city of Seattle. In both regions, growth has rapaciously consumed the natural environment and diminished the human community. The citizens of Greater Vancouver and/or of Seattle may disagree on what is possible for their respective futures; however, there is a growing understanding that we cannot continue to spread ourselves endlessly across the countryside, to live by and for our automobiles, to produce tons of waste and pollutants for every man, woman, and child. We are sucking up all our planet's energy and natural resources, and we are letting our established communities wither. This charrette, however, and the James Taylor Chair in Landscape and Liveable Environments, radiates a fundamental optimism. They declare that we can restore, integrate, humanize, and diversify both the built and the natural environment. Lester Brown of the World-watch Institute has said that sustainability has a better chance of working in our region than anywhere else in the industrialized world. If we can't achieve the proper balance between the built and natural environment, between public and private, and between growth and stability, then perhaps no region can. To not at least try is to follow Los Angeles and Jakarta into the abyss. The James Taylor Chair and the fruits it will bear are predicated on the belief that the right land use, the right transportation system, the right design, at the right scale, will go a very long way towards solving society's problems. To be sure, these strategies cannot solve all our problems in one fell swoop; on the other hand, there is neither the time nor the money to solve them one at a time. It is clear that any solutions will require comprehensive policies and designs – the kind that you will read about in this book.

Doug Kelbaugh, FAIA
Professor of Architecture & Urban Design
University of Washington
Seattle, WA

February, 1996

CONTENTS

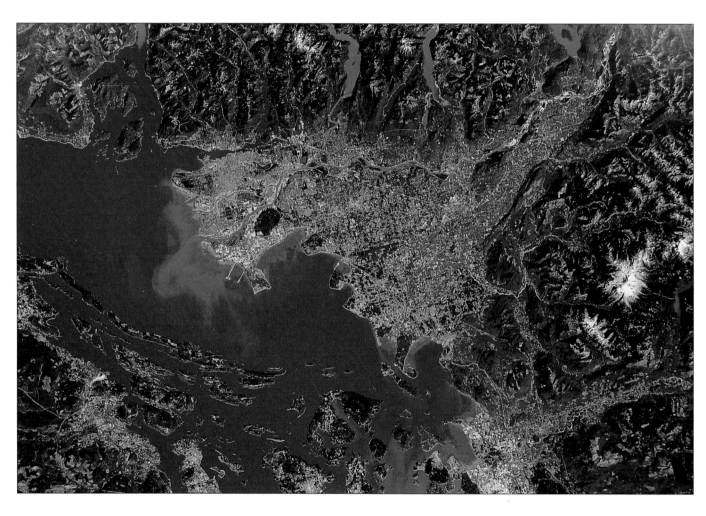

The site:

The Lower Mainland Region of British Columbia as seen from space (this and all other plan views in this document shown with north up). Heavily urbanized areas appear grey. The City of Vancouver occupies the peninsula at the extreme left, bounded by the Burrard Inlet on the north and the Fraser River on the south. The Fraser River divides the urban area, Vancouver and Burnaby on the north shore while Delta and Surrey are on the south shore. Surrey's most populated area appears as the grey region just south of where the Fraser River turns to the southwest. The site is at the south end of this expanding urbanizing area and is identified by a red dot. Large un-urbanized zones lie to the east and to the south of the study site; these are the flood plains of the Serpentine and the Nicomekl Rivers respectively.

INTRODUCTION

PATRICK M. CONDON

The Purpose of This Book

This book is about how to make our new neighbourhoods more sustainable than they are now. By sustainable, we mean the maintenance of the ecological health of our neighbourhoods and the provision of equitable access to affordable housing for our children. We hope that this book will be of interest to everyone; from the public officials and private developers who participate in developing and managing the urban landscape today to the secondary-school students who will shoulder these responsibilities tomorrow. The book includes four different designs for the same 400-acre site in Surrey, British Columbia, each design having been produced by a team of architects and landscape architects, working "en charrette."

Each team had a clear goal: to *illustrate a vision* of what our communities could be like if they were designed to conform with emerging regional, provincial, and national policies for sustainable development. Currently, there are very few examples, or *illustrations,* of what more sustainable urban landscapes could be like. In British Columbia, many ministries and other sectors of government are developing policies and legislation aimed at enhancing the sustainability of future developments. This project was the first in British Columbia to *illustrate* the changes that these policies might bring to the texture and pattern of the urban landscape, should they be carried out. We hope that these illustrations will enhance public discourse by allowing citizens and decision-makers a chance to assess for themselves what a more sustainable urban landscape might look like.

The James Taylor Chair in Landscape and Liveable Environments

This charrette project is the first in a series of related projects sponsored by the University of British Columbia's James Taylor Chair in Landscape and Liveable Environments.

UBC formed this endowed chair in response to the 1987 United Nations World Commission on Environment and Development. In its assessment of the state of the global biosphere, the commission argued that the solutions to global environmental problems lay largely at the local level and, particularly, at the site-development level. Members of the Landscape Architecture Program at UBC realized that most ongoing research in landscape sustainability was being done at the ecosystem scale (landscapes larger than 3,000 square kilometres) and that very little work was being done at the *site* scale (landscapes of less than two square kilometres). In 1990, the Landscape Architecture Program presented a proposal for an endowed research chair in sustainable site design. In 1991, during the UBC's "World of Opportunity" campaign, the university received a gift to endow the James Taylor Chair in "Landscape and Liveable Environments." A central principle that informs all the chair's activities is this: the individual site, and even the individual house and yard, are to the landscape region what the single cell is to the human body. Just as the health of the human body is dependent on the health of all of its cells, so the ecological health of a landscape region is dependent on the health of its individual sites.

A Brief History of Design Charrettes

Most people are not familiar with the word "charrette." A charrette is a design activity where the participants are assigned a very complicated design project and are expected to bring it as close to completion as possible within a very short time. Members of the School of Architecture at the Ecole des Beaux-Arts in Paris coined the word at the end of the last century. The faculty in that school would issue problems that were so difficult, few students could successfully complete them. When the allotted time had elapsed, a pushcart, or, in French, a *charrette,* trundled past the drafting stations. Students would throw their drawings into the cart in various states of completion, as to miss it meant an automatic grade of zero. It was in a similar environment that the participants in the Sustainable Urban Landscapes Design Charrette produced the designs and illustrations contained in this book. We gave them only four days to design a hypothetical community for 10,000 persons in Surrey, British Columbia. The "cart" came by at 7:00 AM on Friday, 15 September 1995, the morning of the presentation, and the designers threw their drawings into it. Those drawings are the ones reproduced on the following pages.

The charrette recorded in this book is not the first one since the nineteenth century; rather, it is one in a long series of charrettes held since the tradition began. In our own Georgia Basin Region, the University of Washington's Department of Architecture has been conducting major design charrettes for more than a decade. In these charrettes, many design topics have been explored, from the reuse of decommissioned military installations to the design of portable water closets for Seattle's homeless. One of the publications emanating from the Seattle charrettes that has influenced urban designers around the world is *The Pedestrian Pocket Handbook,* edited by Doug Kelbaugh and now in its fifth printing. As Professor Kelbaugh had organized all of the Seattle charrettes, we asked him to act as our advisor for this project and to participate as a team leader in our first charrette.

Early in our planning, Professor Kelbaugh cautioned us that the results of a charrette are always unpredictable. He told us to hope for the best but to prepare for the worst. He also encouraged us by stressing the one great advantage of the charrette model: it is the best way to get the most creative proposals for addressing the most difficult problems from the most accomplished designers in the most compressed period. In no other way would (or could) these individuals come together to stimulate each other, teach each other (and their student partners), and compete with each other to produce the best possible answers to a given design problem. An important cautionary point must be made, however. Given the short time in which they were accomplished, *no one* should think of the designs produced at this charrette as complete. These designs are beginnings, not ends. They provide a point of departure for later contemplation and elaboration. In short, *they provide the pic-*

tures of what a more sustainable future might be like – nothing more.

The Specific Goal of This Design Charrette
The goal of this project is to demonstrate what our neighbourhoods and communities could be like if they were designed and built to conform with emerging local, provincial, and federal policies for sustainable development.

We expect these policies will emerge and develop a great deal more in the future, as we learn more about the possible avenues towards increased landscape sustainability; but the first step towards a sustainable urban landscape is to accept and to work with these emerging and existing policies and to draw pictures of what it would look like. We do not believe that these policies by themselves guarantee sustainability, they do not; but it is clearly worthwhile to make the first step by illustrating their potential benefits.

The above-stated goal suggests the following more specific objectives:

1. To produce sustainable community design models for real British Columbia urban landscapes
2. To illustrate the design consequences of meeting disparate and often contradictory sustainability policy objectives
3. To illuminate the connection between sustainability and livability
4. To show how sustainable design objectives are influenced and/or impeded by typical community subdivision and site and traffic engineering regulations
5. To create a setting in which leading British Columbian designers can exchange ideas and viewpoints with outside experts in the field of sustainable design
6. To produce design proposals that may provide patterns, processes, and prototypes for other Georgia Basin communities
7. To broadly distribute the results of the charrette through a variety of means and venues – to citizens, elected representatives, policy-makers, students and designers – and thereby influence future public policy and legislative initiatives

The Process of Choosing the Charrette Site
Early in the planning phase of this project we presented the charrette idea to participants at the November 1994 meeting of the Greater Vancouver Regional District's[1] (GVRD's) Technical Advisory Committee, which is comprised of the senior planners from GVRD communities and other com-

munities in the region. The committee also includes representatives from the relevant provincial ministries and Crown corporations. We invited the participants to submit candidate sites from their communities for consideration, and five different Lower Mainland communities submitted a total of thirteen potential sites.

The Sustainable Urban Landscapes Design Charrette Advisory Committee then reviewed these thirteen sites. The committee selected the 400-acre site in the South Newton District of Surrey because it has several physical and cultural characteristics common to many other communities in the region. The committee also felt that Surrey's leading elected officials and its citizens were committed to preserving the natural beauty and ecological integrity of their city as it grew. The combination of physical site characteristics and an interested public made the 400-acre site in Surrey a logical choice for the first charrette project.

The City of Surrey is very large, 126 square miles, making it, physically, the largest of all Lower Mainland communities. It has a population of 294,000 and is growing by 4 to 6 percent per year. If this rate of growth continues, Surrey's population could surpass that of Vancouver, presently British Columbia's most populous city, in the year 2021. While a quick glance suggests that Surrey has a substantial amount of land available for building new neighbourhoods, closer examination shows that almost half of its land lies within the boundary of the protected Agricultural Land Reserve (ALR). These undevelopable lands are the low-lying flood plains of the Nicomekl River and the Serpentine River. An even closer look shows that the "buildable" upland areas of the city are laced with protected salmon-bearing streams, which are very important to the ecology and aquatic productivity of the region. In summary, although there are enormous demands for increased development in Surrey, its remaining land base is crucial for habitat and local food production. We hoped that participants, through presenting intelligent designs, would be able to demonstrate ways to mitigate this potential conflict.

The 400-acre charrette site includes upland regions and low wet areas. As such, it provides a representative cross-section of the surrounding city. The site is divided into sections by important salmon-bearing tributaries of Hyland Creek. It is located at the edge of a recently urbanized area – the Newton District – and is one of the next logical catchment areas for Surrey's population expansion. The city

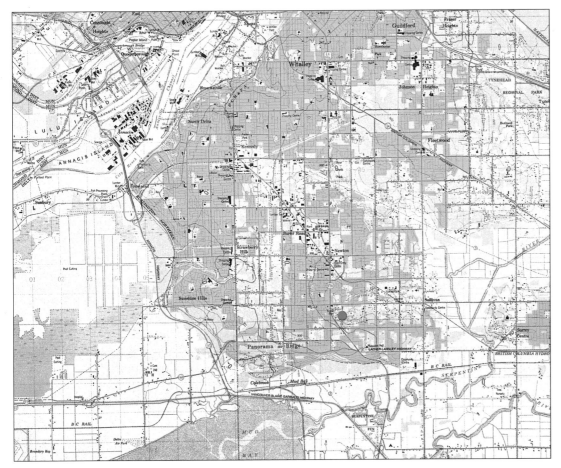

Left:

A topographic survey map showing the study site in its context. The study site is again located by a red dot. On this map, presently urbanized areas are shown in pink, forests in green, and agriculture in white. The Serpentine and Nicomekl Rivers, to the east and south of the site respectively, are bordered by wide agricultural flood plains. These flood plains divide Surrey into three distinct upland urban zones: (1) the Newton/Whalley/Guildford urbanization, to the immediate north of the study site, (2) the Cloverdale District, ten kilometres due east of the study site, and (3) South Surrey, seven kilometres due south of the study site.

Below:

The four-hundred-acre charrette site. Boundaries of the study site are shown with a heavy black line. This part of Surrey is drained by the Hyland Creek and its tributaries. The main stem of Hyland Creek forms the northern boundary of the study site. Several of Hyland Creek's smaller tributaries dissect the study site. Hyland Creek and its tributaries are clearly marked in the photo by the long lines of forest vegetation. King George Highway forms the western border of the site. Sixty-Fourth Avenue lies close to the northern edge of the site while 60th Avenue lies close to the southern edge of the site.

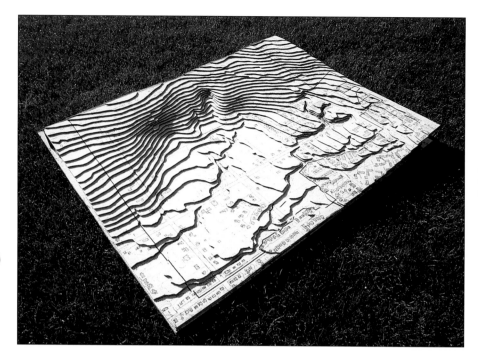

Left:
Topographic model of the site as seen from the northeast. Vertical change has been exaggerated by a factor of two for clarity. Stream channels are shown by the linear depressions. Groundwater emerges from many locations near the base of the slope to feed the streams. The high southern edge of the site is part of the much longer Panorama Ridge formation. The soils on the site are of glacial origin – generally unstratified deposits containing a high percentage of clay.

is presently planning to "upzone," or increase, the allowable density in the area to accommodate this next wave of population growth. Approximately 980 persons live in the area today. Most of the site is privately owned, with parcels ranging between ten acres and one-quarter of an acre in size. Real estate investors own many of the parcels, and, generally, they are anxious to see the land "upzoned," since this would dramatically increase the value of their holdings. Resident home-owners own most of the remaining parcels, and they generally enjoy the natural qualities of the site and are not anxious to see it change. The home-owners that we spoke to had little doubt, however, that change is inevitable; but they hoped the city could preserve the qualities of the site that they most enjoyed. Slopes on the site are quite moderate by local standards, ranging from 13 percent to 1 percent. The site is an inward-focussed bowl shape, with ridge-top parcels enjoying very good views to the east and north. Nine different threads of the Hyland Creek system incise this site.

The Charrette Program Brief
The charrette planners derived each element of the design brief[2] by carefully culling the various sustainability policy statements of a variety of government or quasi-government sources published since 1990. If we felt that a policy objective had clear implications for site design, we used it to guide the design program. For example, we arrived at the 10,000 minimum

population after studying a set of inter-related policy objectives, all of which supported relatively high-density development. These policies included goals such as "accommodating walking distance access to services and transit," "creating affordable housing," "using developable land efficiently," and so forth. This process ensured that the design illustrations would truly *demonstrate what our neighbourhoods and communities could be like if they were designed and built to conform with emerging local, provincial and federal policies for sustainable development.*

In short, the program required the designers to find a way to house at least 10,000 persons on the 400-acre site, while preserving or enhancing the ecological function of the land and the surrounding landscape. We knew that it would be very difficult to fit that many people on the site and still preserve or enhance the existing ecology. We believed that this kind of challenge would bring forth the designers' most creative responses, and we were not disappointed. We also asked designers to provide unusually large amounts of commercial and light industrial space. The designs would thus reflect "complete community" planning principles (i.e., they would provide enough employment and services within walking distance to drastically reduce the time, energy, and money consumed by driving).

The Composition of the Design Teams
Two professional landscape architects and two professional architects led each team.

Each team included an even mix of architecture and landscape architecture students from the UBC School of Architecture and the UBC Landscape Architecture Program. Half of the team leaders were drawn from the region, and the other half were invited from other parts of North America. The leaders were chosen for their recognized accomplishments in urban design, their experience in similar venues, their understanding and commitment to the principles of sustainability, their capacity to work quickly and cooperatively, and their ability to work with students. With equal numbers of architects and landscape architects on each team, the design dialogue was intensified.

Conclusion
We hope these designs enhance the discussion about sustainable urban landscapes. We believe that by drawing pictures of what a more sustainable urban landscape could be like, public officials, developers, and citizens will be able to make more informed decisions than they do at present. The four designs included in this book all represent practical ways to make our urban landscapes much more sustainable than are our present ones. We feel that they are economical, safe, and attractive alternatives to status quo suburban development. We also feel that they accurately reflect how the urban landscapes will change as the emerging sustainability policies for our region are actualized.

We hope, too, that this book illustrates the importance of design in the quest for sustainable urban landscapes. In our charrette, it was *design* which first revealed and then resolved the contradictions embedded in the sustainability policies used to guide the design brief. For example, the design brief required that the community be both densely populated (to conserve energy) and ecologically preserved or enhanced (to protect the streams). Reason suggests that you cannot do both these things at the same time. Neither science nor planning, by themselves, can overcome this seeming contradiction. Scientists agree that when a site is changed, even in the simplest way, the ecological consequences are not completely predictable; the relationships between the various systems are simply too complex. As you add urban uses to a site, the number of variables approaches infinity. Issues of sustainability and ecology are thus inherently complex, and science falters when confronted by so many variables. Design, however, is quite at home with complex problems, for even the simplest design problem has many variables and many acceptable solutions. Often these acceptable solutions are pleasing and practical in proportion to the designer's success in balancing the contradictions embedded in the design problem. Design may not be able to find the absolutely *correct* solution, but, when such a solution is not possible, it can find a number of *very good* solutions. Four very good solutions to the problem of urban landscape sustainability are bound between these covers.

One closing point: the solutions in this book may tell us how to move towards urban landscape sustainability, but they do not lead us all the way there. However, even moving *towards* sustainability requires dramatic changes to the status quo. If history is any guide, it could take many decades to significantly change old ways of city-building. But we should at least begin. We hope that the design visions illustrated in this book will contribute to that beginning.

Patrick M. Condon, ASLA
James Taylor Chair in
Landscape and Liveable Environments

Notes:

1

The Greater Vancouver Regional District (GVRD) is a provincially enabled public agency that is, among other things, charged with coordinating growth in the Vancouver metropolitan region. Certain of the key documents informing the design program were produced under the direction of the GVRD, notably, *The Livable Region Strategy* and *The Livable Region Strategic Plan*.

2

The complete program is included in the appendix, and careful review of it is recommended.

Top:
Aerial view to the east from above the western edge of the site. The Public Market building, located at the intersection of 64th Avenue and King George Highway, is prominent at lower left of the photo. The charrette site occupies the foreground and the middleground of the view. The flood plains of the Serpentine River and the Cloverdale district of Surrey are in the distance.

Bottom:
A typical view from within the site. This view is to the north from the upland southern edge of the site. The encroaching urban development of the Newton District can be seen on the ridge in the middleground. The North Shore Mountains, thirty kilometres to the north of the site, are visible in the distance.

The Sustainable Urban Landscape

Below:

The beauty of the quilt illustrated depends on the contrast between the strong order of its pattern and the organic quality of its fabric. Our community design is analogous to this. The beauty of the *urban quilt* depends on the contrast between the strong order of its pattern of streets and lots and its natural systems.

Artist: Merrill Mason Title: Tornado III Photographer: Carina Woolrich Courtesy of Quilt San Diego

TEAM ONE

Ken Greenberg
Jennifer Marshall
Bill Wenk
Don Wuori

There is a fundamental dialectic which occurs on sites such as this 400-acre site in Surrey. On the one hand, we have the image of Arcadian nature, an organic softness; on the other hand, we have the tools of the surveyor, the grid line and the cardinal point. In the twentieth century, the later has held sway over the former. Nature has been seen as a nuisance, something we try to overpower when we develop a site. On any site, the natural systems (topography, hydrology, vegetation, and so forth) are its most important structuring element. Yet our system of cutting up the land into parcels takes no account of natural systems, and Surrey reflects this bias. The entire city, including this site, is broken up into quarter mile or 400 metre by 400 metre sections, each section containing 40 acres. As the countryside becomes the city, these 40-acre squares get cut up into 20-, 10-, 5-, and 1-acre squares. The one-acre squares are further broken up into $^1/_2$, $^1/_4$, $^1/_8$ acres, and so on.

This system of cutting squares often obliterates the Arcadian qualities that originally brought new residents to these suburban landscapes, but it doesn't have to be this way. Our team hit upon the image of the quilt and decided it would be a useful metaphor for our site plan. In a quilt, you have the organization of the grid, much like the organization of the surveyed landscape, but you also have the colour and pattern of the materials, much like the natural systems of the site. A quilt is beautiful and functional to the extent that its organization and its materials are in harmony. Similarly, we feel that this site is beautiful and functional to the extent that its ordering systems and its natural systems are in harmony. What we are looking for is an intense touching, integration, and interaction between the two.

Working Within the Pattern

We began by accepting the pattern of ownership on the site, which is, of course, a reflection of the surveyor's grid, and we imagined how it might evolve, over time to become the "urban quilt" we were hoping for. Our plan shows a snapshot of the site taken, say, fifteen years from now, when the individuals within those various parcels are beginning to change the site by adding housing, institutions, schools, shopping, jobs, and so on, in such a way that the patterns of nature are not suppressed but are rather expressed and emphasized.

The strength of the pattern of nature in our design is largely a consequence of individuals respecting the natural processes of the site when they change it; in particular, respecting the way that rainwater moves through and out of the site. Rather than sterilizing the site by removing rain water as quickly as possible through the use of expensive, heavy drain pipes and inlets (structures common to almost all newly developed areas), this community is designed to respond to the water. We found ways of absorbing and containing the water that fell on the site, allowing it to percolate back into the ground, back into the water table, and slowly back into the natural systems. Not only does this process naturally clean and slow the water moving off the site, it also offers a potential savings of millions and millions of dollars by obviating the need for heavily engineered storm-drain systems.

Our next move was to extend the natural forest of the stream-ways by linking it with the urban forest of the new and existing streets. This uniting of the cultural landscape with the natural landscape is a key element of our urban quilt. It functions to both visually and actually integrate the ecology of the streams into the ecology of the community.

Connection, Not Separation

Our third move was to emphasize *connection* over *separation* in our transportation system. Current practice for planning suburban communities emphasizes separation over connection – residential streets separated from collector streets, collector streets separated from arterials, and so on. While this pattern may reduce through-traffic on cul-de-sac residential streets, it has an unfortunate side effect; it greatly increases the distances required to get anywhere, leading to greatly increased dependence on the automobile. The arterial streets that serve the area quickly become overloaded, requiring ever greater expenditures to widen them until, finally, they become great barriers between districts. We suggest reverting to an older pattern, the pattern of the

Left:
Team 1: (back row) Jennifer Marshall, Richard Peck, Bill Wenk, Don Wuori, Ken Greenburg, Nick Sully; (front row) Sai-Hong Lai, Launie Burrows, Jurij Sennecke, Jennifer Nagai, Cheryl Machan, Dan Abboud; (not shown) Suzanne Pearson

interconnected grid (which is quite common in all the older Vancouver neighbourhoods). A connected grid system can carry much more traffic, with all trips made by a more direct route, than can the disconnected cul-de-sac to arterial system. This increased capacity reduces the strain on the surrounding arterial roads, allowing them to function as commercial centres that join, rather than divide, adjacent neighbourhoods. In our plan, community services are dispersed, and are never more than a five or six minute walk from your home. The car is no longer king. If this pattern of development were to be adopted throughout the province, we could achieve major savings in energy use and major reductions in pollution.

Our next point has to do with the ecology of the housing stock. Just as diversity is a positive attribute of a working ecosystem, so diversity in housing type is a positive attribute of a working community. Diversity of housing type allows the community to fit the ecology – low-density single-family housing in the forest preserves, high- and mid-density housing where the landscape allows for it. There are a diverse number of human needs and family types in our modern world, and this diversity is reflected in this plan – duplexes next to fourplexes, fourplexes next to apartment blocks. In this community, you will not be forced to move far away when you leave your parents' home, when you are a single parent, or when your children are all grown. There is a place for everyone here.

The site we were given has 162 hectares, out of which, when you remove all of the streets, parks, and natural systems, you are left with about 96 hectares of developable land. We have preserved some thirty hectares of that land in the form of parks and open spaces, which exceeds by a substantial amount the minimum requirement for open space specified in the design brief. We provided some 7 hectares of land for retail, commercial, and industrial space as well as $4^1/_4$ hectares for institutional spaces of various kinds. Many institutional spaces (i.e., churches, libraries, and so forth) are mixed into residential zones. We are conservatively assuming that about 15 percent of the people living in this community will have home occupations and our building types have been selected on this basis. The approximate number of dwelling units at full buildout would be between 2,800 and 3,500 units, which would allow for a population of 8 to 12,000 people. This works out to between 30 to 35 dwelling units per hectare on the developable lands. This is a reasonable density, which allows most

people to occupy freehold houses with their own lots and their own gardens. Thus, we feel that we have successfully resolved the contradiction between the ecological imperatives and the density requirements of the design brief. We feel that the "urban quilt" of our design, pieced together by respecting both the cultural patterns of the city *and* the natural patterns of the land, provides the means to overcome this contradiction.

Certainly this plan demonstrates what the Surrey site could be. It also suggests what might happen if the principles built into this plan were to be adhered to throughout the region: The network of natural systems would be protected, but, more than that, the natural systems would start to play a role in shaping our communities. The stream beds could become the natural and recreational corridors of our neighbourhoods, preserving the natural qualities that brought people to Surrey, the "City of Parks," in the first place. Thus, this "urban quilt" may be seen as a single square in the even larger quilt that this region could someday become.

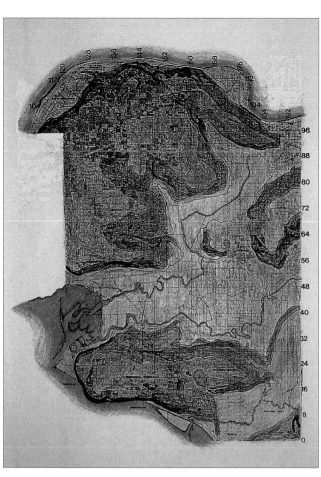

Left:
Diagram illustrating the major landforms of Surrey and the stream system that drains them. Steeper slopes are shown in the darkest shade of green; lowland flood-plain regions are shown in the lightest shade of green. The middle shade of green shows upland headwaters regions, where most of the present population of Surrey resides.

Below:
Early map of Surrey, showing how the city was cut into "sections," each section numbered and its owner listed. Note that the pattern does not acknowledge differences in natural features, such as topography and drainage-ways.

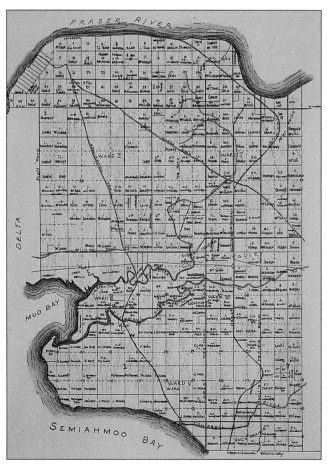

Below:

This drawing shows the gradual process by which the original forty-acre sections are usually subdivided. At the last stage of this progression, the interior of the original forty-acre section is filled with houses and cul-de-sacs. The pattern shown in the fourth drawing is typical of most of the urbanized areas built in Surrey after the Second World War.

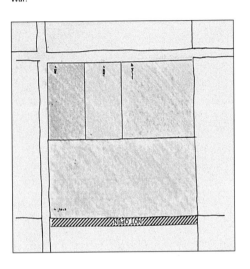

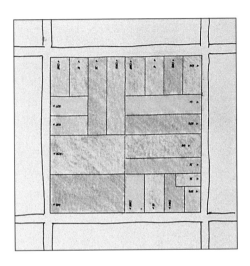

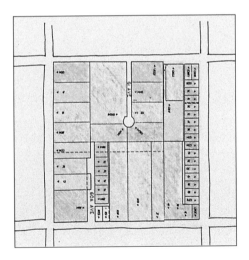

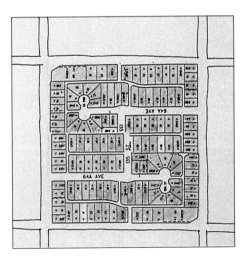

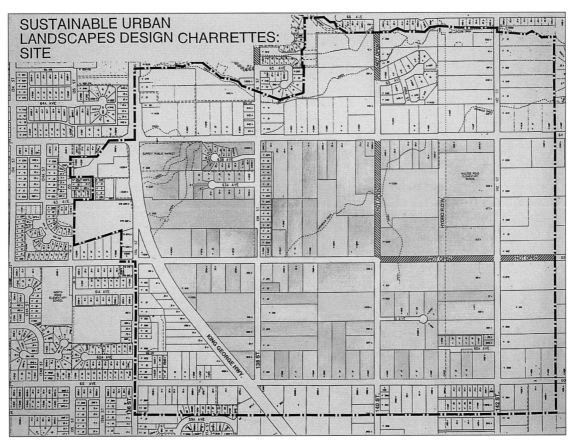

SUSTAINABLE URBAN
LANDSCAPES DESIGN CHARRETTES:
SITE

Above:

Present ownership pattern on the study site. The site is presently at the third stage of the subdivision process charted in the previous illustration. Without a change in policy, it will soon resemble the fourth stage in the previous illustration.

Right:

Diagram illustrating how water would be collected at street edges and brought overland to the edge of the stream. During a normal rainfall, storm water would be held at the top of the stream embankment until it could percolate down through the soil.

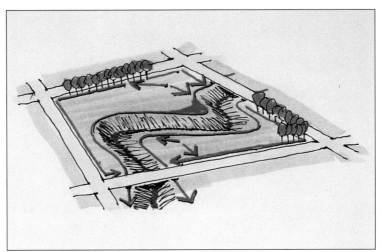

Below left:

Schematic diagram of the storm-water system. Water moves along road verges (along the straight lines) to the top of stream banks. Water then moves parallel to the stream to holding areas (shown as large blue dots), where it percolates through the soil and/or is held for slow discharge back into the stream.

Bottom left:

The proposed street system for the site respects the existing pattern of forty-acre sections and surrounding roads but adjusts it to fit the natural systems. All roads connect to other roads. Trip distances for cars, people, and bikes are as short as possible. Low-volume roads are shown in blue, medium-volume roads are shown in red.

Below right:

Forest vegetation in the streamways (shown as blue winding lines) is preserved. Stream vegetation is re-enforced by the preserved or planted groves in the large recreation areas (dark green). Tree-planting along the streets completes the system and provides a continuous thread of green for the new community (straight lines of blue dots).

Bottom right:

Services are available at the four corners of the site. Thus, no resident would live more than a five-minute walk from transit or services. Large rings show the distance from service centres that most people can walk in five minutes.

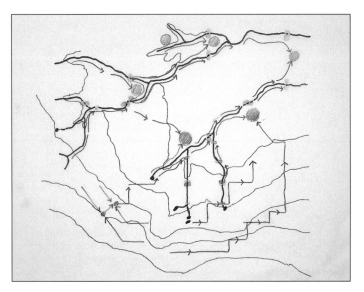

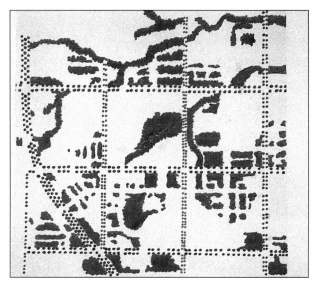

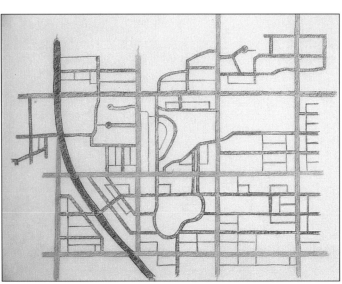

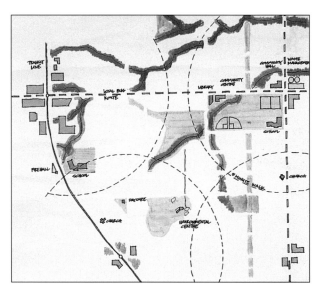

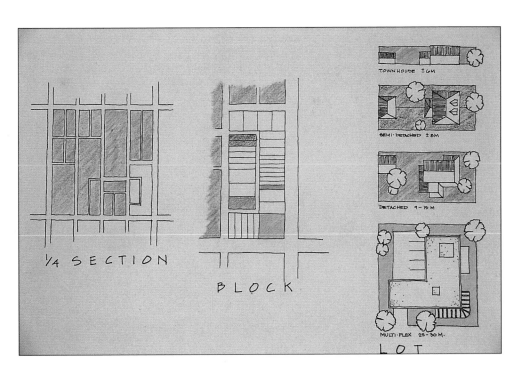

1/4 SECTION

BLOCK

LOT

TOWNHOUSE ± 6M

SEMI-DETACHED ± 8M

DETACHED 9 - 15 M

MULTI-PLEX 25 - 30 M.

Left:
This diagram shows how the existing pattern of ownership within the quarter sections could gradually evolve into the complex, inclusive, and connected system promoted in our proposal. Only a few changes to current municipal regulations would be required in order for this evolution to take place.

Below:
Many different types of dwelling structures are discernible in this figure-ground diagram of the structures proposed for the site.

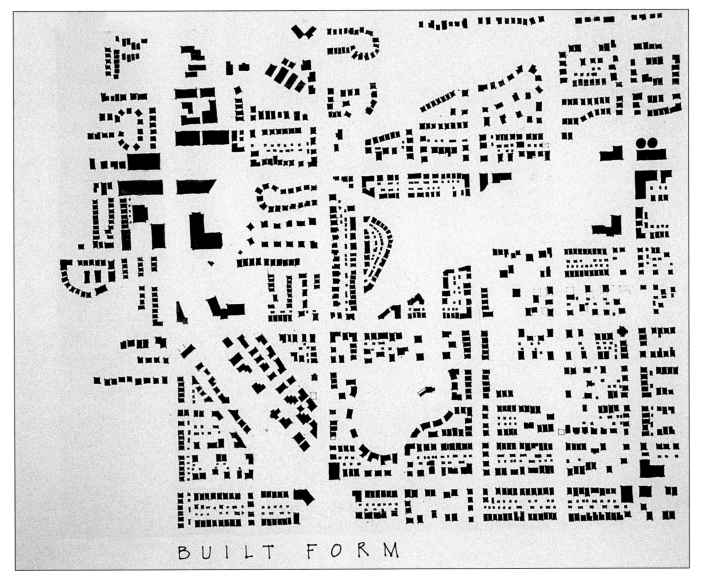

BUILT FORM

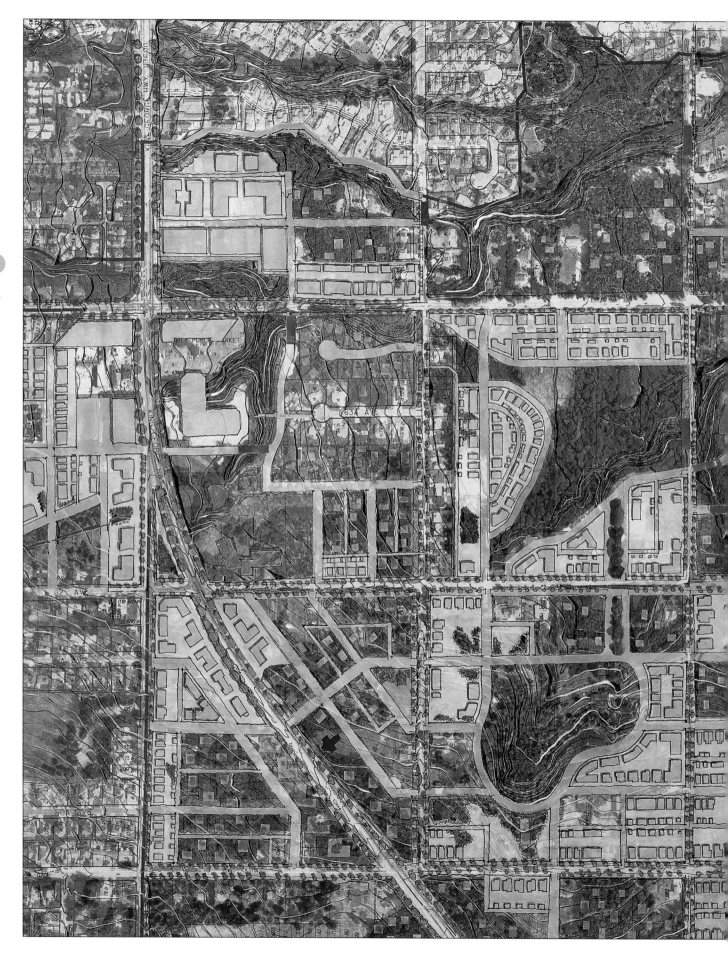

Left:

Site plan of the Urban Quilt. The existing pattern of owner-ship is respected, and the most sensitive parts of the site are preserved. The natural systems of the site have played an important role in shaping this community. The site plan shown is a snapshot of the site at some future point in its ongoing evolution.

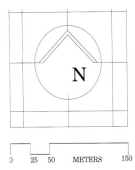

0   25   50   METERS   150

Right:
The site as it appears now in an aerial photograph.

Below:
A drawing of what it might be like ten years from now. The new road pattern is in place, and the public recreation and natural area system has been established. Certain neighbour-hoods are shown at full density. Commercial centres are shown in red.

Left:
Perspective view of one of the high-density residential areas situated at the edge of a natural area. Presently, natural seepage of ground-water occurs just below where the street edge is shown. Here, and at other locations in our proposal, the natural ground-water system has been incorporated as a positive feature of the design. This enhances the ecological function of the site, saves construction costs, and avoids such problems as flooded basements.

Left:
View across King George Highway at 64th Avenue looking east. The necessarily wide highway has been made pedestrian-friendly. Street trees merge with stream corridor forests in the distance.

Left:
Typical view down one of the residential streets on the site. Note that the houses are close to the street to preserve space and to enlarge backyards. Side yards are also small in order to preserve land. The paved surface is narrow as it is in older neighbourhoods. Note the natural overland drainage system in the grassy roadside swales typical of rural communities. This helps to clean the water before it is returned to streams.

Below:
View of the central recreational area, with the residential neighbourhoods shown in the background and the stream channel shown in the foreground. Note the informal holding ponds/wetland areas that parallel the stream and are divided from it by the walking path. Also note that the bridge that crosses the stream has been designed to allow for the easy migration of fish and animals up and down the stream channel.

29

Team One

The Sustainable Urban Landscape

Right and far right:
Two topographic maps of the same area. The one on the immediate right shows the area in its present state; the one on the far right shows the area as it would be if this proposal were in place. Note that in the second map the natural systems become obvious features of the site. This contrasts with the surrounding urbanized districts, where the original natural systems have been obliterated. Also note how the pattern of interconnected roads in the study-site area differs from the pattern of separation and segregation in the surrounding urbanized districts.

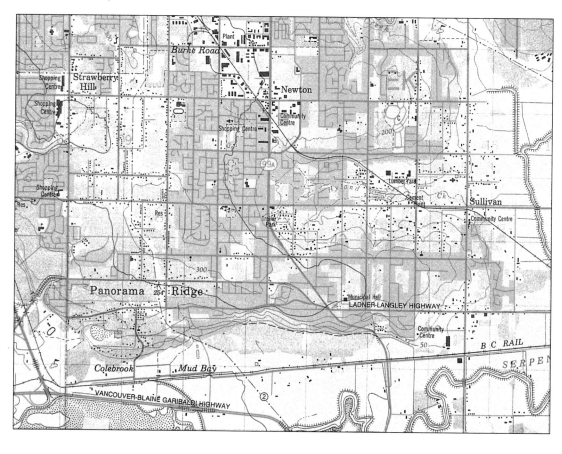

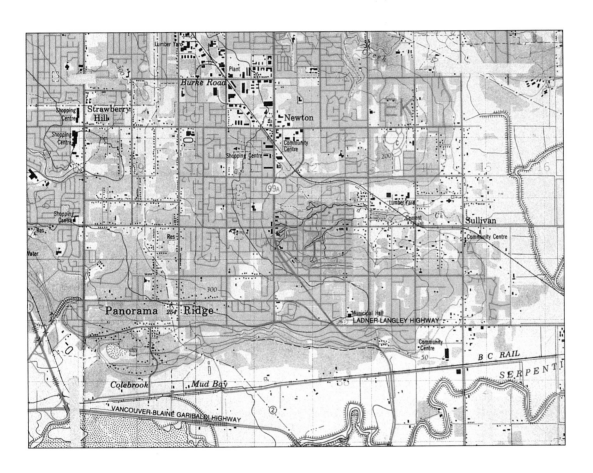

Below left:

High density land-use is not antithetical to shady, pedestrian-friendly districts, as demonstrated by this Vancouver neighbourhood scene. High-rise buildings can be good neighbours to single family homes and vice versa. Accepting this principle, Team Two included a full range of lot densities in their proposal for the study site.

Below right:

A picturesque and sustainable lane-way, lined with private gardens, in an existing Vancouver neighbourhood of detached homes. The site shown has a residential density greater than thirty dwelling units per acre. Team Two revised and renewed this tried-and-true city block pattern in their proposal for Maybeline.

TEAM TWO

Joost Bakker
Cheryl Barton
Doug Kelbaugh
Stacy Moriarty

THE CONCENTRATED CENTRE

The design for a community of 10,000 in Surrey began with a study of the existing physical characteristics of the 400-acre site and its landscape context. We studied the cultural and ecological patterns on and around the site and began to understand them as comprising the evolving context for our community design proposals. The *biological landscape systems* of streams, wetlands, soils, topography, and natural vegetation were studied along with the *cultural patterns* of roads, hedgerows, orchards, fields, woodlots, drainage-ways, utilities, and ownership patterns. To this evolving context we brought some explicit values and design principles.

First, we placed a high value on enhancing the function of the site's biological systems. The streams, wetlands, woodlands, meadows, soils, and topography are all part of the headwaters of the Serpentine River and are characteristic of the upland areas of Surrey. The ecological health of the river valley has already been compromised by existing development; we proposed to design a community that would reverse this trend.

Second, we brought to the project a concern for the people who would be living in this community. We tried to put ourselves in the places of the people who live in Surrey and to create a place for single people, groups, and families. Just as with our concern for a healthy and diverse biological system, we placed a high value on the possibility of creating a healthy and diverse human community.

Principles for Sustainable Design

We came to this project with a few agreed-upon principles for sustainable community design. The first principle is this: The sustainability of a community is related to the cultural and ecological health of the region in which it is located. The most logical and achievable physical manifestation of this principle, and a major feature of our design,

is the *concentrated centre.* This is a place where people can live in large numbers, shop, access community services, and find satisfying work. In the concentrated centre, we find most of the advantages of our traditional regional centres, only confined to a much smaller site. Our prototypical centre, presumably one of a series, is linked to the region via the proposed light rail line or other transit system on King George Highway and by the already highly developed road network that intersects at this site. A series of distinct neighbourhoods are then planned around this centre. Given their proximity to the concentrated centre, services and community facilities are within walking distance of each home or apartment in the community.

The second principle is to make the community a distinct and unique place. We feel that a healthy community should be full of choices and differences. Consider for example the wide range of housing types we proposed for the community – from tower and four-storey apartments to townhouses, duplexes, fourplexes, and single-family houses with and without secondary suites. Here, no one will be forced to leave when family circumstances change.

The third principle is especially germane to this particular site. This site is an important part of a larger system, which depends on clean water for its health. Our community is designed to fit in with the larger system of animals, plants, soils, and waterways that surround it. Our community is designed to *enhance,* and to *coexist* with, the natural systems of the larger region.

When we thought about these three principles together, we came up with a street and open-space system that was especially good at accommodating a variety of housing types, was economical to build and to maintain, could be easily built over time, could support an overland storm-drainage system, and could actually improve the ecological function of the site. We worked to show how such a neighbourhood could be green – through the planting of boulevards, through the provision of neighbourhood parks, and through allowing space for private gardens. We also found a way to conserve all of the streamways, wetlands, and many upland meadow areas. We saved enough of these various types of habitat in adjoining parcels to help meet the local and regional need for wildlife habitat and clean water.

The Broken Grid

Our proposed pattern of streets, lanes, and blocks conforms to the major street and parcel lines already on the site. However,

Left:
Team Two: (back row)
Louise Boutin, Doug Willoughby,
Cheryl Barton, Graham Coleman,
Doug Kelbaugh, Joost Bakker,
Stacy Moriarty; (front row)
Graham Elvidge, Gurinder
Grewal, Paul Etheridge,
Lee Beaulieu; (not shown)
Denise Burtch

rather than superimposing a continuous grid over the entire site, we broke it at the stream corridors, wetlands, meadows, and woods. Breaking the grid in this way produced a community pattern of smaller neighbourhoods gathered around the large central green space. In certain locations, where the neighbourhood grid is broken, the street crosses the green space in the form of bicycle and pedestrian pathways. These "green streets" link the neighbourhoods with the community centre.

The neighbourhood grid provides a secondary system of surface waterways that directs, retains, and infiltrates storm-water on the site, thus enhancing the water quality of the stream system. Roofs, yards, streets, lanes, and roadside swales were modified to create this drainage system. A gravity-fed biotechnical sewage treatment system is located at a lower elevation of the site to clean grey water before discharging it into the stream.

The broken grid results in some interesting and unconventional parcel configurations where natural areas pre-empt streets, homes, and yards. Although not the stuff of a surveyor's or developer's dreams, these oddly shaped parcels provide such essential services to the community as (1) shallow retention basins to slow runoff into streams, (2) community garden areas, (3) woodlots and berry fields, and (4) neighbourhood parks – all of which greatly enhance the ecological function of the district and enrich the neighbourhood atmosphere.

One Day in the Life

To give you a sense of how it all fits together, we would like to take you on a "day in the life" of a member of this new community. And, since every community needs a name, ours is called Maybeline. We had a lot of trouble coming up with a name for our community, first considering, then discarding, names like Hyland Centre, King's Market, Surrey Market, Frog Hollow, Slurry Hollow (because we talked a lot about sanitation and sewage), Sludge Hollow, Green Grid, and True Grid. Ultimately, we chose Maybeline because, although it referred to absolutely nothing, it is memorable.

If you are lucky enough to live in Maybeline, you would have a much wider choice of housing stock than is presently available in suburbia. Let's say you are the breadwinner and you live in a single-family home down by the creek. You have a quick breakfast in the kitchen while looking out the back window, through which you see a two-car garage with an apartment above it. It could be a "granny flat" (a small secondary suite); it could also be a home office, a

teenager's lair – you name it. As you look at it, you remember that your oldest has recently gone off to college. He was living in it and it's now time to think about getting a tenant. So you remind yourself to stop at the municipal hall later in the day to pick up a rental application.

You leave through the front porch. It's just a few steps down to the path, and about ten feet to the sidewalk. There are front porches on all the houses, and all the front yards are small. There is a sidewalk, which is not often the case in suburbia. As you walk to town, you pass a neighbourhood park. This neighbourhood park includes a small day-care centre along with the usual paved courts and turf playing fields. You turn along tree lined streets that lead to the centre; it's a very green and shady neighbourhood. Let's say you're walking to the centre to pick up your transit connection to work. As you go through this network of streets you can always get where you want to go by the shortest route possible, almost "as the crow flies." After about a five-minute walk you arrive at the town square, which has a hotel and a major municipal building. There is a music tent, and you remember that there is going to be a concert that weekend.

On up through the centre of town you go, past a large market that serves not just Maybeline but lots of folks who hop off, and back on, the trolley. As you pass by the office buildings, you wonder what on earth the architects were thinking when they put these steel and glass towers right next to a traditional-style farmer's market! You cross a bridge and go down onto the platform to wait for your train. While you're doing that, you can have a cup of coffee, buy a paper, and talk on your cellular phone. You notice, though, as you look out, that there's this channel, this corridor, where King George Highway has been narrowed down. Although this is an extremely pedestrian-oriented community, the joys of driving have not been forgotten. The automobile driver speeds along a roadway which is lined on both sides with flashy electronic signs and mirrored glass buildings. Your tram arrives and you jump on. Your commute takes about twenty to thirty minutes.

After work you come back; but before going home, you cross the bridge to the high-rise neighbourhood, where it seems that mostly seniors have chosen to live. One of your former neighbours sold her house and moved up to the "loft," as they call it. You go and see your mother-in-law because you need to pay a bill for her. As you go up to the fifteenth floor and out

onto her balcony, you realize that this is one of *the* best views in Surrey. You can see southeast to Mount Baker and south and west to the Georgia Strait. You are on some of the higher land and these are the highest buildings in this part of the region. This and other buildings built recently along the spine of Panorama Ridge form an impressive sight. Sometimes, when the sun hits them just right, like last month when you were coming back home after doing business down in the States, it takes your breath away.

Back across the bridge you go. You walk down the main street in the shadow of the towers, stopping at the market to pick up fresh fruit, flowers, bread, and the odd sundry item that you might need. The market is big enough to house a movie theatre; however, it's not a mall, it's a public market, which is an important distinction. It has all the life and vitality typical of public markets, particularly in this region, which is so famous for them. You stop at the municipal building, where there's an auditorium; but you're just paying a bill this time. You quickly scoot out and, as you go by the King George Inn, you stop and make a reservation at the fancy restaurant that overlooks the park. Then back to your house, using the lane this time so that you can check on your car and get a map. Motoring is now a lot more pleasant than it used to be. There aren't as many cars on the road these days, so you are planning an automobile trip for the weekend. You might stop, though, and have a convivial chat with a neighbour (who is sitting on her front porch) before you go into the alley.

The Standard of Living and our Quality of Life

It's a very walkable, pedestrian-friendly, slow-paced district. But none of these pleasant green neighbourhoods can be sustained without having the mixed-use, transit-friendly compact centre nearby. In our plan, we have about 4,000 people living within 2,000 feet of the transit stop. Those high densities are what makes the lower densities on the rest of the site possible and, indeed, keeps other parcels of land throughout Surrey and the region undeveloped. These tight nodes served by transit are the essential element of a more sustainable landscape. Driving uses far more energy than does heating, cooling, and lighting buildings. So, although many of the buildings in our plan are energy efficient because they have party walls, solar greenhouses, and party floors, the amount of energy used in the ten automobile trips the typical family takes per day is far greater than what it could possibly use to heat or cool its home. When your goal is cutting energy consumption and air pollution, you have to cut automobile trips. We calculate that this urban pattern can cut the number of trips per day by more than half, and it can cut the miles driven per person per day by even more than that.

Finally, we spent a lot of time looking at the existing landscape. It is, in fact, a very beautiful landscape, but it is a wolf in sheep's clothing. Lurking under that green carpet are lots of hidden costs and lots of hidden problems. It's not a sustainable landscape environmentally, socially, or economically. If we were to pay the true cost of gasoline and land, few people could afford it. It's also heavily subsidized and is bankrupting the local and provincial governments. If we insert a much denser node into the picture, then we can allow much of the green to stay green. Getting 10,000 people on 400 acres is four or five times the norm. That means that for every square mile developed along the lines of Maybeline, you can save four or five square miles of green.

A final important point: It is probably true that our *standard of living*, as measured purely in terms of consumption, will decline during our children's and our grandchildren's lifetimes, as the Third World takes its fair share of the world's resources. But we also think that their *quality of life*, as measured in terms of health, social stability, access to decent housing, and leisure can actually improve. If this happens, we think it will result in communities that look a lot like Maybeline.

Below:
The design for Maybeline evolves from integrating the layers of the site in a way that expresses and enhances the function of each layer. Layers are either ecological or cultural: land, water, vegetative pattern, or public infrastructure.

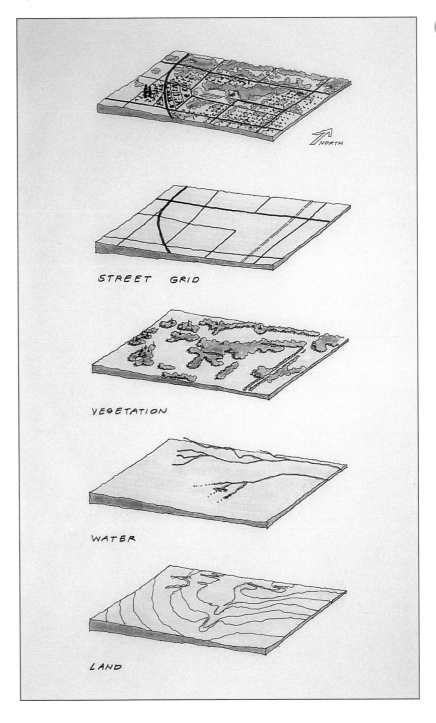

STREET GRID

VEGETATION

WATER

LAND

Right:

Illustrative plan for the site. Commercial uses are shown in light red, high-density housing is shown in orange, low-density housing is shown in yellow, and public and civic buildings are shown in blue. The concentrated centre is located at the lower left (the southwest) corner of the site. Four thousand persons live in the concentrated centre, which is built around a proposed transit station on King George Highway. Six thousand persons reside on the other portions of the site. A neighbourhood grid of narrow streets and lanes has been integrated with the existing pattern of highways, rural roads, and rectangular lots. This grid gives way when confronted with the natural stream areas. The major east-west connection through the middle of the site, 62nd Avenue, becomes a pedestrians and bicycle route. The stream areas provide a natural storm-drainage system and a frame-work for neighbourhood civic and recreational facilities. Neighbourhood schools, day-care centres, and play areas are located within the natural areas at the centre of the site. A grey water treatment centre is located at the northeast corner of the site.

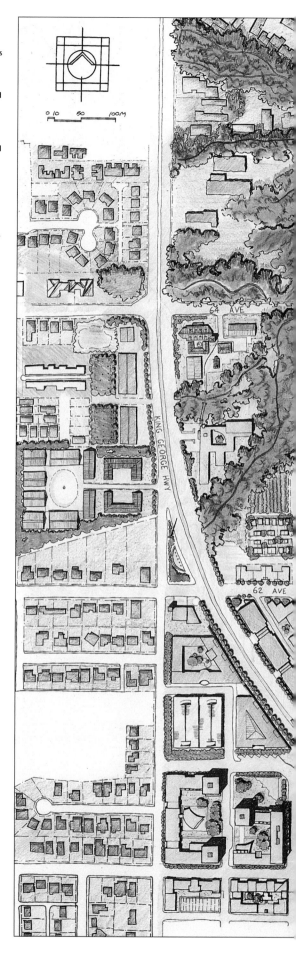

Right and top far right:
The most common tile in the regional mosaic is the "quarter mile section," containing forty acres of land. This site, and most of Surrey, is gridded off in quarter-mile sections. Using this quarter-mile section as a frame, we were able to develop three neighbourhood design strategies, variations on which are applicable in many communities. The first one, shown at the top of this page, is four blocks wide and six blocks deep, which results in 240 by 300 foot blocks. This is a tried and true, very walkable pattern that has worked in many countries, including Canada. With these narrow frontages, it makes sense to have lanes or alleys out back to access the garage. Thus, no on-street parking spaces are sacrificed to driveways, and the dominance of garage doors on the streetscape is eliminated. If there are rental units over most garages, you can achieve a density of about twenty-three units per acre. The sketch shown at the bottom of this page shows a four block by five block pattern, which produces slightly larger blocks and deeper lots. The deeper lots create more opportunities for lane housing. The diagram at the top of the opposite page shows the four by four block pattern, which has the highest density. The lots, as shown, are deeper and wider than is the norm, which opens up additional housing options. With these patterns you can achieve populations of 2,000 to 3,000 people in each quarter-mile section. This number can support a commercial area within walking-distance and has a population density which makes public transit economically viable.

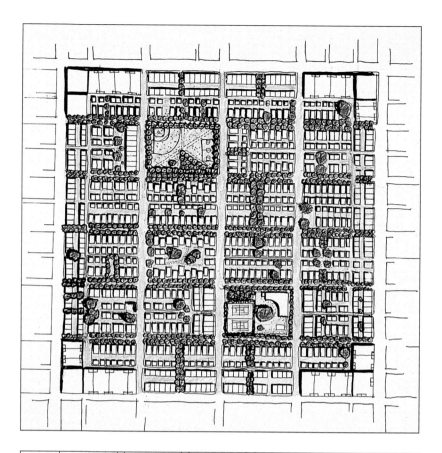

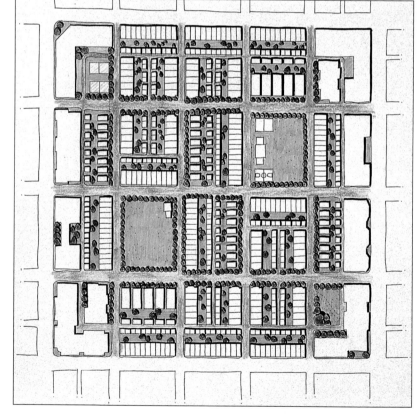

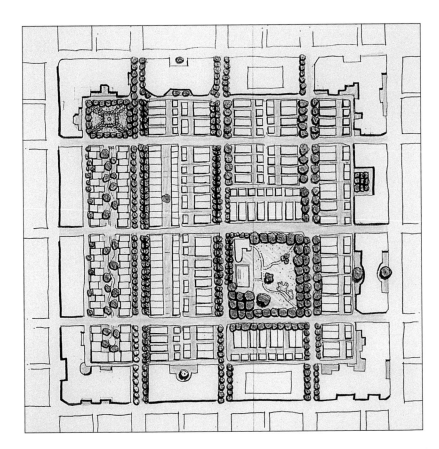

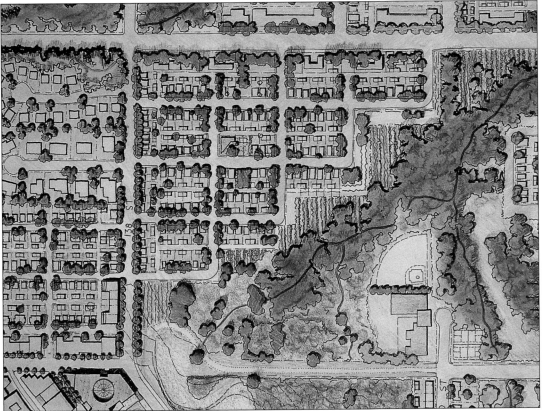

Left:
A detail from the illustrative site plan showing a portion of one of the gridded neighbourhood districts. High-density residential is located astride the busier 64th Avenue. Certain civic functions, such as the church/assembly hall (shown in blue), are integrated into the interior of the neighbourhood. The residential grid is interrupted for the stream corridor. Community gardens are located between the neighbourhood and the stream. Recreational trails traverse the stream corridor. A community school (also shown in blue) and its associated recreation area is located near the stream and conservation area. Grassy meadows surround the mown playing fields, adding to the habitat value of the play area.

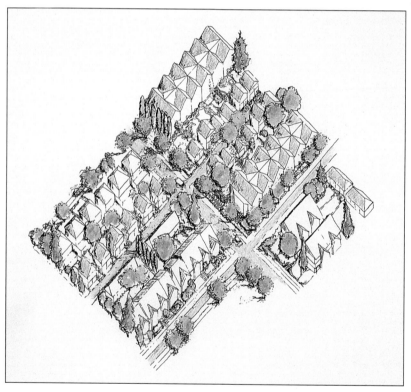

Left:
Two explorations for narrow residential streets. Narrow streets save more land and have slower traffic than do wide streets; they are also less expensive, create fewer ecological impacts, and are easier to shade with street trees. The examples shown allow parking on gravel verges. Drainage is kept on the surface and is directed to roadside swales. Versions of the example shown on the left are common in many of Vancouver's older neighbourhoods.

Below:
Perspective view of a typical street in Maybeline. Houses with porches come up close to the street, on both sides of which are sidewalks and boulevard plantings. Streets are narrow. Note the natural area at the end of the street; in Maybeline, almost all residential streets terminate at one of the natural stream areas.

Below:
In certain locations in Maybeline, streets bridge streams. Bridges are required (rather than culverts) because they prevent damage to sensitive fish habitat. They could be old-fashioned one lane bridges (as shown) in order to slow traffic, reduce environmental impact, cut expense, and provide a pedestrian scale.

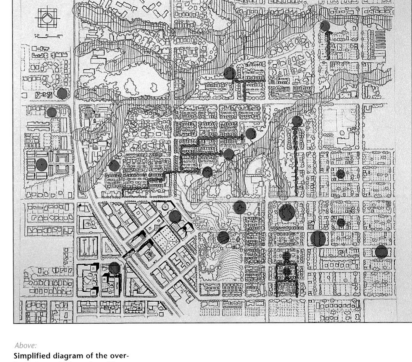

Above:
**Simplified diagram of the over-
land storm-drain system. The
storm-water is channelled overland in roadside swales (shown
as blue dashed lines), to de-
tention areas (shown as large
blue dots). From there, the clean
water is slowly released back
into the nearby stream.**

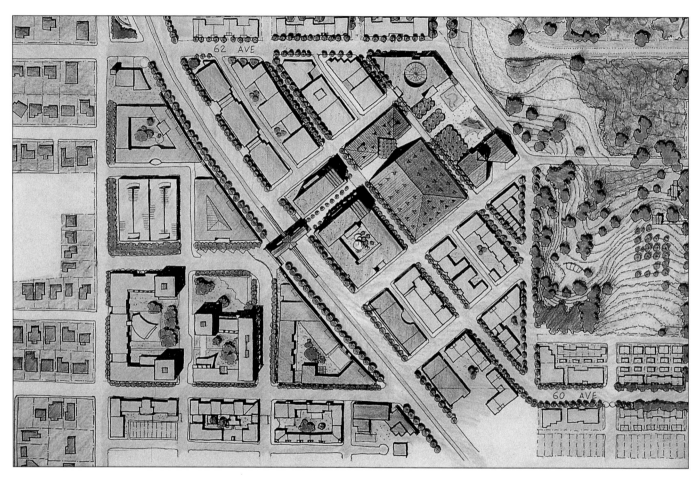

Above:

Detail of the concentrated centre from the illustrative site plan. The high-rise neighbourhood is at lower left and is connected to the main centre via an elevated pedestrian bridge shown crossing King George Highway. The main transit stop is located under this bridge, and paired office towers are located at its northeast end. The large rectangular building next to the office towers is the community market. Four-storey residential buildings occupy the sites to the northwest and the southeast of the towers. The smaller building (tinted blue) is for municipal and social service functions. A public square provides the setting for these buildings and connects the concentrated centre to the central park and the stream system to the northeast.

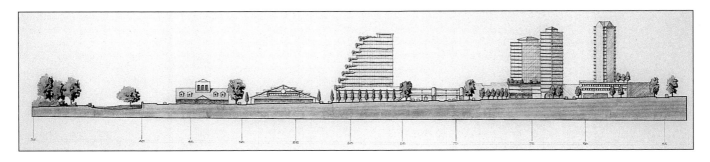

Above:
A sectional view through the concentrated centre. From left to right are the public park, the public services building, the public market, the office towers, King George Highway (with the pedestrian bridge and transit stop), and, at the far right, the high-rise neighbourhood.

Below and right:

The study site as it appears now is shown on the left. While the site is attractive in its present state, it is not sustainable. It is heavily subsidized and its real costs are unaffordable. The design for Maybeline is shown on the right. Development of this site (and many others in the region) in accordance with the sustainable principles developed in this design will preserve more green space, reduce dependence on the automobile, provide more affordable housing, and improve the ecological function of the region.

Below:
Images of Hyland Creek taken at the site. Team Three made special effort to preserve the natural ecology of the site, the streams and the stream habitat of the site in particular.

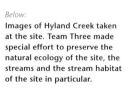

TEAM THREE

Ray Pradinuk
Moura Quayle
Murray Silverstein
Ron Walkey
Carolyn Woodland

It is obvious that Surrey is at a fork in the road. Its lands are beautiful and resource-rich, and choices abound for their stewardship and for a new city form. Which path should we follow? This scheme is about the significance of the site to the region and of the region to the site. Our particular site is of both local and regional ecological significance because it contains the headwaters of Archibald and Hyland creeks and their many tributaries, all of which are important salmon-spawning streams and drainage ways.

Historically, Surrey's uplands and ridges were covered by forests, peat bogs, and marsh lands that acted as sponges to control water discharge. Increased run-off from the highlands has contributed to lowland flooding and erosion. Water retention is poor in Surrey, and aquatic systems will decline as new development takes over vegetation, habitats, and creeks. This can happen quickly, so we should take these issues seriously.

This scheme explores four basic ideas: (1) the addition of 2,200 dwelling units by 2015, (2) the creation of a town centre, (3) the nurturance of the evolving ecology, and (4) the location of dense, mixed-use buildings at the edges of the site. We understand that Surrey is growing, and our proposal will provide a new community at King George Highway and 64th Avenue at a pace and a density that the ecology and the location can withstand.

We are interested in promoting a "not-so-fast" attitude to development. Rather than develop in big chunks to an arbitrary maximum all at once and all the same way, our team recommends that the community be built in smaller increments, a little at a time, when and wherever the need is felt, and in the very particular way that each site suggests. In other words, do not just discourage, *disallow*, large land assemblies.

This community needs housing of different types for people of different incomes and ages. As a result, we propose establishing a pedestrian-scaled town centre at King George Highway and 64th Avenue. To make it a real centre, we have to repair the urban fabric of the three other surrounding quarter-sections and the ecological fabric of its fourth – our site. To nurture the delicate site ecology, we recommend placing in reserve just over one-half of the study site as a "regenerating woodlands." This 200-acre landscape should be given over to community use and stewardship. A healthy regional water system, water retention, vegetation regeneration, and the maintenance of rural traditions are a few of the considerable benefits that would accrue from this move.

Circulation and open space are important. One basic problem with traditional suburban development models is that neighbourhoods are cut off from their own centres of public life. All that is needed to repair them, though, are a few simple road and path connections designed to create an integrated network. Many kinds of paths and roads are needed in a community: "calmed" major streets; car trails; regional and local greenways for cars, bicycles, and pedestrians; and woodland footpaths and boardwalks. We do not need to increase the capacity of roads that bleed our communities of places to work, places to gather, and places to shop that are within walking distance. We are saying, for example, that 64th Avenue should not be widened. Instead, build a greenway, a sort of ecological parkway for walking, biking, cars, and transit that takes you all the way to Langley! We are also saying that a lot of small roads can serve a community better than can one giant road.

If this site is to continue to contribute to the sustenance of our regional ecology (e.g., through providing healthy salmon habitat), we must be extremely mindful of its ecological function. For example, there should be special emphasis on the site's water systems. The site's ecological function was the basis of our decisions about its development potential. In our plan, Archibald and Hyland creeks can support diverse habitat while still draining the site.

The Regenerating Woodlands
Roughly half the area of the site is regenerating woodlands. Emanating from the arterials that surround the site, development threads towards its woodland centre. The move to line the arterials with pedestrian ways and high-density development is based on our belief that we cannot continue to turn our backs on pedestrian use of both arterials and major collector roads. These streets should be places to live and

Left:
Team 3: (standing) Lynda Carabetta, Moura Quayle, Murray Silverstein, Omar Nagati, Yolanda Leung, Wendy McWilliam, John Shupe, Ray Pradinuk, Wayne Palchinski; (sitting) Ron Walkey, Carolyn Woodland, Kirsten Bartel, Adam Vasilevich; (not shown) CEJ Mussell

work, not just places to move through. Threaded through the regenerating woodlands is a lacework of intimate laneways. We propose that these laneways be dense and urban at the edges and loose and picturesque as they become paths in the forest. If one did live on these laneways, choices for movement and activity would abound. Some mornings a walk into town to go to the library, buy a paper, and have tea would be appealing; other times, a bicycle ride through the woodlands to the market garden at Archibald Creek Commons or a talk with the district arborist about the care of the trees in the common would be on the agenda.

The key question is: How do you build a community bit by bit? Let us look at years 2002, 2009, and 2016. We start with what is there now, and we make sure we leave room for what may happen, and what we might want to happen. And, in 2002, the site will not have changed so much, even though more people will be living there. The same houses that line 64th Avenue will still there – maybe the same families will still be living in them. Even after fourteen years, most of the same places will still be there. By this time, the social and community mechanism for sustaining the landscape will be more clearly understood. More people will realize that the health of the watershed improves when "users become stewards." Replenishing these landscapes will be a part of everyday living, as will be ensuring that they are cared for at the community level.

All around the woodlands, a community will be building. The Archibald Creek Commons will be in the heart of the woodlands, easily accessible by bicycle, and there one may find a stewardship house for land and nature programs. Adjacent to the commons, along the greenways, will be a community school, assembly hall, a chapel, and a horticultural work-yard. The commons is the focus of maintaining rural traditions through all forms of land management (e.g., such as productive nurseries, gardening, reforestation, family farms, and rural-based businesses).

King George Highway and 64th Avenue
In the town centre, we propose a mix of commercial, public, industry, and housing uses. The same incremental approach is possible in both residential areas and in the town centre. Over time, the density of the area changes, and the richness and diversity of the community emerges. The centre includes many places to both live and work; numerous small workshops and offices open out onto the sidewalks and the

small public squares. The greenway and path system is also integral to the success of the town centre since it connects the town centre to the community it serves.

The regenerating woodlands and the proposed town centre at the intersection of King George Highway and 64th Avenue have served as examples of our vision for this community. It is important to note that we have not accommodated the expected 9,000 people on this site that the design program called for; our population number was closer to 6,000. Our recommendation is that the town centre and the already low-density developed area to the west and north of our site should be "repaired" and "densified" to accommodate more people and services. This repair should not be confined to the urban sector; it should include natural sites. We need to provide richness, diversity, and increased density in all of the over 100 square miles of neighbourhoods that have already been developed in Surrey.

In summary, we want to create a new living and working environment at the urban edge. We want to bring the landscape into the routines and patterns of everyday living by developing an integrated network of roads, paths, and green corridors. We also want to increase landscape diversity and, at the same time, intensify the use of key developable areas. In other words, new development should be seen as an opportunity to improve stream health, to rebuild ridge recharge areas, and to strengthen green corridors.

Our message is: build, yes; however, at the same time, repair the city and the natural ecology in a way that allows them to co-exist.

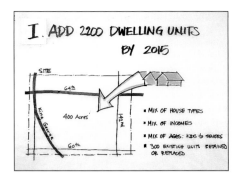

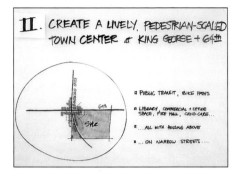

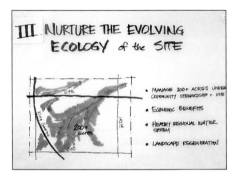

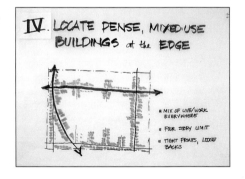

Left:
Four fundamental principles that underlie this urban design.

Below:
The study site in the context of Surrey's stream and river system. Colours indicate regions of ecological sensitivity. Ecological sensitivity information is taken from the 1990 City of Surrey Environmental Sensitivity Assessment (ESA) study.

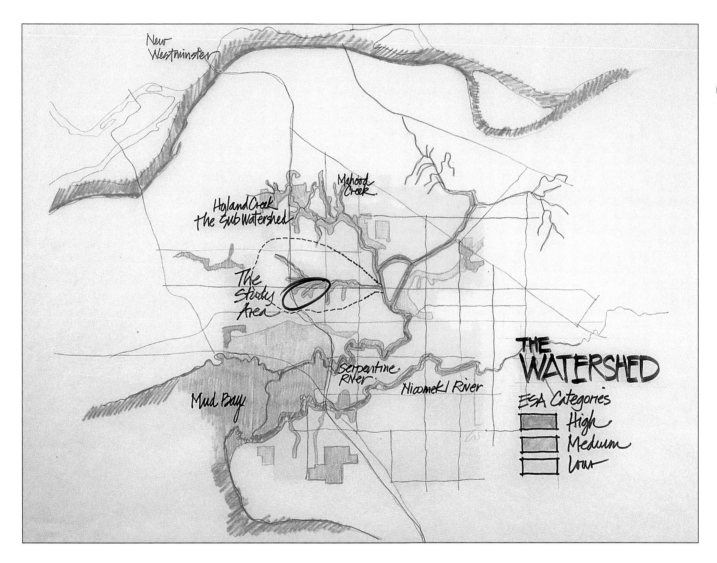

New Westminster

Mahood Creek

Hyland Creek
the Sub Watershed

The Study Area

Serpentine River

Nicomekl River

Mud Bay

THE **WATERSHED**
ESA Categories
High
Medium
Low

Left and right:
Pathways are always available to connect different parts of the site. Bike and pedestrian travel is given priority. A system of laneways and paths takes the place of the usual wide suburban street. The path and street network points to, but then skirts, the most sensitive parts of the site. The pattern established in this district can be extended to the surrounding districts over time, as is indicated in the plan of the larger district on the right.

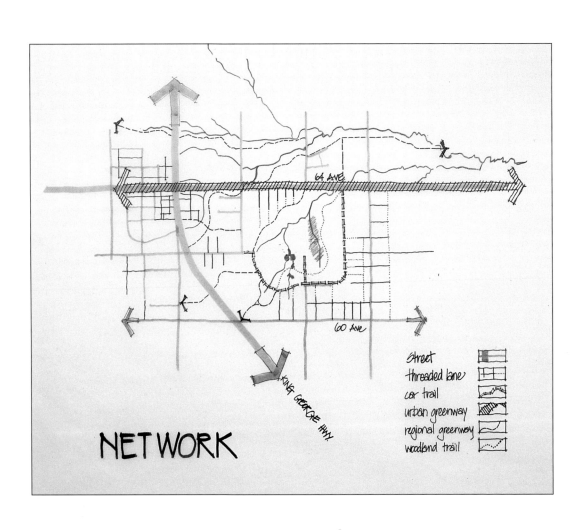

NETWORK

Street
threaded lane
car trail
urban greenway
regional greenway
woodland trail

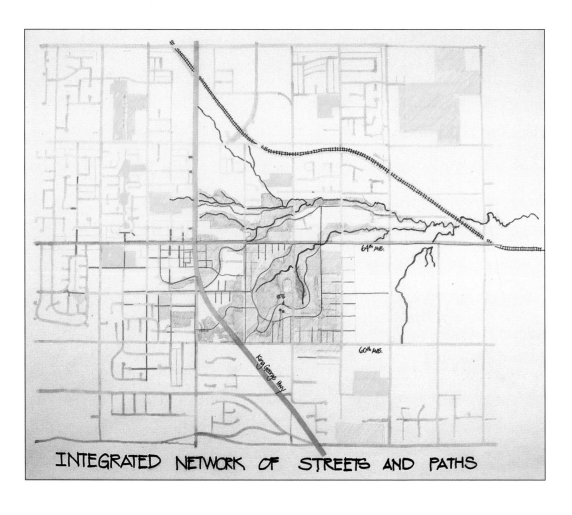

INTEGRATED NETWORK OF STREETS AND PATHS

Right:

Plan of the site as it might appear in the year 2016. High-density commercial, light industrial, and office buildings (shown in bright red) line King George Highway. One Hundred and Forty-Second Street provides another suitable location for high-density construction, this time for housing and related commercial and civic uses. Low-density residential enclaves migrate towards the centre from the periphery. The centre of the site is dominated by conservation lands. Stream channels are given very wide buffers, and bike and footpaths are integrated with the streamways. Community facilities are located near the natural areas. The Archibald Creek Commons is located in the exact centre of the site. The school and community facilities complex is grouped around the large open clearing near the intersection of 64th Avenue and 142nd Street in the northeast quadrant of the site.

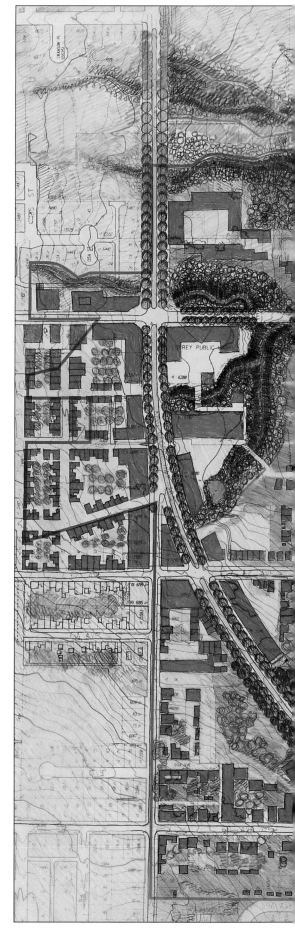

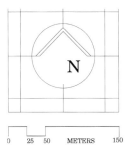

N

0   25   50   METERS   150

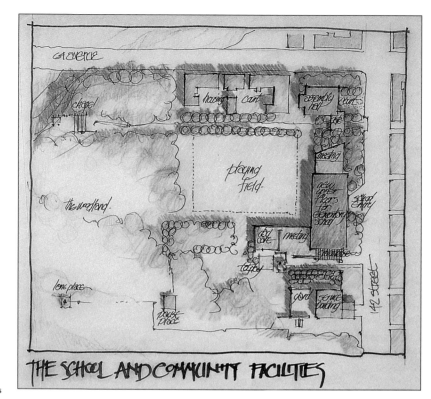

THE SCHOOL AND COMMUNITY FACILITIES

Top:
The school and community facilities site in the northeast quadrant of the site. This area provides facilities for housing, services, and schools. The existing school has been expanded to accommodate the new residents and day-care and elderly services are located near each other.

Bottom:
The Archibald Creek Commons is located at the centre of the site. This community centre complex resembles a small farm. Many of the activities planned for this space focus on agriculture or sustainability. The community centre is most easily accessible from all areas of the site via footpath or bike path.

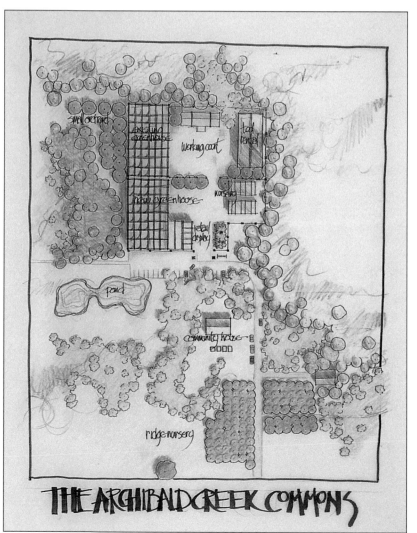

THE ARCHIBALD CREEK COMMONS

Below:
The incremental growth strategy is illustrated by this series of diagrams. Note that the lot configuration does not change. As time passes, residences fill in the rear of the lot. The forest near the stream is allowed to grow out towards the main street, while the houses are allowed to move towards the stream. Eventually, the area is both much denser and ecologically much richer than it was before.

TODAY

YEAR 2002

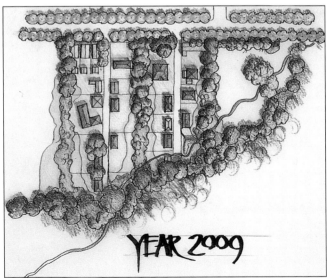

YEAR 2009

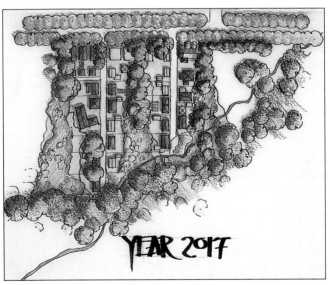

YEAR 2017

Right:

Large increases in density are brought about by placing houses with small "footprints" on narrow lots. The single-family home shown has about 1,200 square feet of interior space on four floors (including the basement) and either two or three bedrooms. The cost of providing this kind of home is about half that of building a home of equal interior area in most suburban locations; because of the present high cost of land and of providing roads and utilities to serve house sites, along with regulations that prohibit small lots, this size single-family home, which is quite common in older neighbourhoods, is now impossible to build.

Bottom:

Even greater density can be achieved with the "duplex" or two-family home. Each family can still have a garden and a home it can afford. This old-fashioned house type was traditionally owned by one family, who rented out the other half. Now, "strata titles" (two or more owners of the same property) are also common. Note the small (400 square feet of interior space) "cottage" over the garage—useful as a home office or as "studio" rental unit.

A HOUSE + SMALL LOT IS STILL AN OPTION.

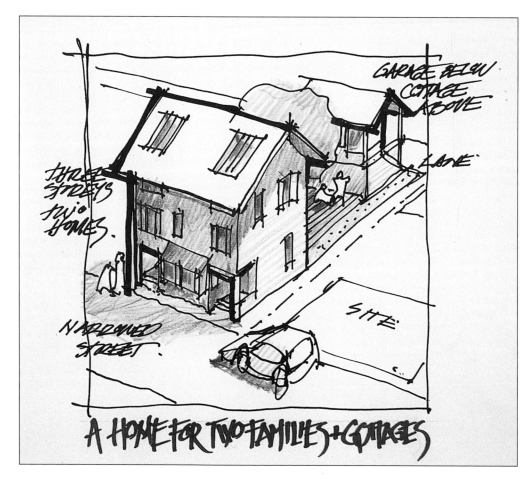

A HOME FOR TWO FAMILIES + COTTAGES

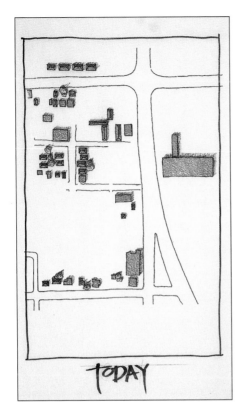

TODAY

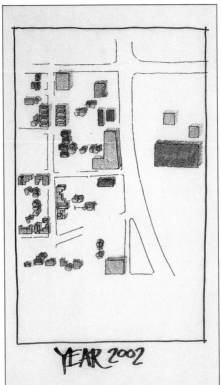

YEAR 2002

Left:
The incremental growth strategy can also be applied to the town centre. Note that the existing buildings are retained and that, as time passes, the large empty spaces begin to be filled in with small-scale, diverse urban development. A series of internal community squares emerge as buildings go up around them.

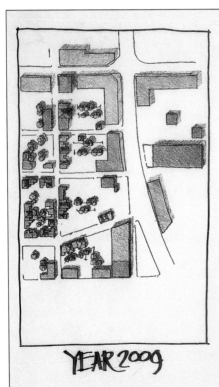

YEAR 2009

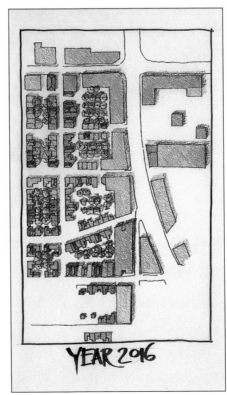

YEAR 2016

Top left:
View to the east across King George Highway near 64th Avenue. Arcades provide a protected pedestrian space while maximizing site density.

Bottom left:
The wide variety of uses that are to be found in the town centre are revealed in this cut-away view.

Below:
Aerial view of the site as it might appear in 2016. View is to the west, with the intersection of King George Highway and 64th Avenue at lower left. The town centre is in the foreground, the conservation area is in the middle ground, and the 142nd Street residential area is in the background.

TOWN CENTER: LOOKING ACROSS KING GEORGE TO THE MARKET

TOWN CENTER: WORKSHOPS ALONG THE PEDESTRIAN PATH

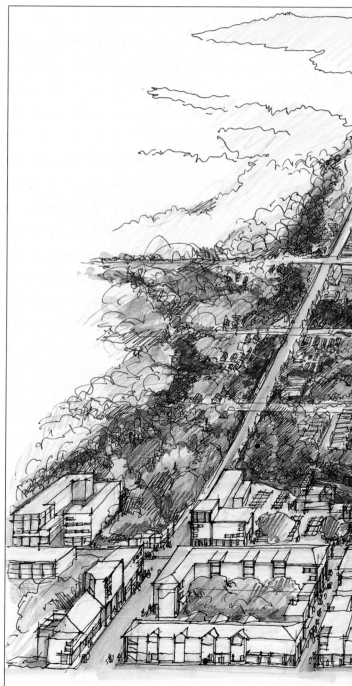

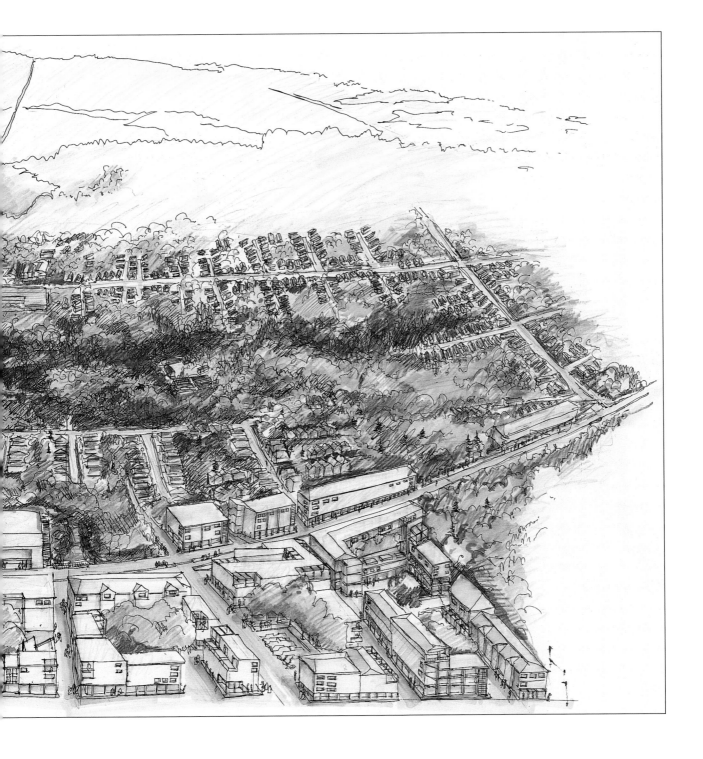

Below:
Quick concept sketches that express the team's preliminary vision for the charrette site and for the larger context. This vision includes ecological, visual, functional, and cultural dimensions. It is a vision of an *integrated,* not a *mitigated,* nature.

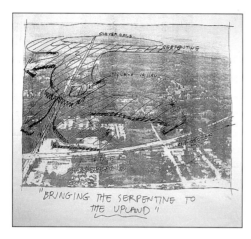

"BRINGING THE SERPENTINE TO THE UPLAND"

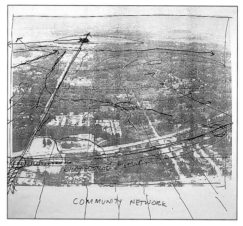

COMMUNITY NETWORK

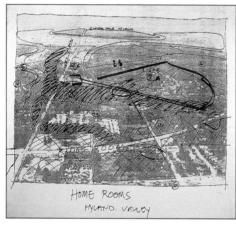

HOME ROOMS
HYLAND VALLEY

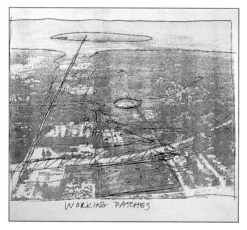

WORKING PATCHES

TEAM FOUR

Catherine Brown
Patrick Condon
Roger Hughes
William Morrish
Don Vehige

THE VALLEY OF TWO WATERS

There are two ways to approach the question of urban landscape sustainability. You can use the design language of "mitigation" and create some sort of benevolent buffer between nature and the city; or you can use the design language of "integration" and try to fuse nature and the city. We chose to use the latter. When you make this particular choice, everybody has to pay attention and work together at a maximum level of creativity. This is not the way it has been done in the past, but we, as a culture, are beginning to discover that integrated urban landscape design approaches to development are essential to achieving urban sustainability. In the past, we have treated nature as that thing that sits out there in the landscape that we put things on. More recently, we are starting to see that nature is not just "that thing out there," but that it is actually something that pushes back when pushed. Recognizing nature's capacity to push back when insulted is important if one is concerned with protecting a region's social and economic vitality. It is good to see this recognition reflected in the urban development policies that are emerging from the regional, provincial, and federal authorities.

In keeping with this principle, in our design we let nature make the first push. Rather than taking the lines of the urban grid and placing them down on the site, hoping they will fit (and if they don't just bulldozing the site or doing whatever it takes), we tried to let the land "push up and out." We wanted to see what would happen if we shaped the zoning principles for the site by responding to the natural features of the land. We started by studying the natural features of the whole city of Surrey. We did this so that we could better understand our own 400-acre site. The first thing that we realized was that the urbanized city covered less than two thirds of the total land area of Surrey; the rest was unbuildable flood plain, protected from urban development by being located within the boundaries of the Agricultural Land Reserve. Only three areas of land are left for urban development, and all of these are on hills surrounded by rivers and farmlands. The second thing we realized was that for Surrey to become a city in its own right, more than just a bedroom community, it couldn't continue to add houses to its highlands indefinitely. The city had to rebuild as it urbanized.

The View Out to the Valley

But how should the city rebuild? During the first part of Surrey's development, the focus was on the headwaters lands, the highest and driest parts of the city. The forest was cleared a little bit at a time and the suburb grew. But now that the suburb is becoming a city and stretching out to the edges of the highlands, this focus towards the high points becomes less important, while the view out – to the river valley – becomes more important. Yet, as far as we could make out, the importance of this river valley had not yet been recognized, at least not from an urban planning or design perspective. In most of the planning documents that we reviewed, the river valley area appeared as an empty white hole, which, in effect, said, "No planning needed here!" All of the planning documents seem to concentrate their attention on the headwaters communities rather than on the river valley itself. Yet the valley is so strong! Strong enough to unify this spread out and almost placeless city.

There is little doubt that, as the city grows, the many edges of the valley will become important communities. When this happens, the orientation of the community will inevitably change from being inward-focused (to the highlands) to being outward-focused (to the lowlands). With this in mind, thinking about how to make that important new connection from the highland to the lowland becomes very important. The city of Surrey's emerging lowland front yard can be treated either pragmatically or with due deference. There are many important points where this connection occurs and could be improved. Sixty-Fourth Avenue, which traverses the northern boundary of our site, is one of the most important of these community connections.

From the Upland to the Lowland

With the contrast between the inward view and the outward view in mind, we asked ourselves the question: Where does our site fit in between the headwaters and the valley? We discovered that our site is a turning point and an entrance point to two powerful landscapes – the upland and the lowland of Surrey. We started to think about the site as, in essence, an "upland-to-lowland" site, and how upland to lowland was a better fundamental planning unit for the site, a better way to characterize it, than as just so many square lots in the grid. This site is not just a bunch of squares on a piece of paper; it is a three-dimensional natural environment. The fundamental notion of a "three-dimensional natural environment" should be used as the basic tool for building this or any other site. With this tool, all land value and density pieces can be connected. Using the existing natural systems of a site to decide what kind of development is appropriate will ensure that those same natural systems are integrated and enhanced and, equally important, that the spatial characteristics of the site are emphasized. Applying this principle to our site, since it was an upland-to-lowland site, it made sense to make the upland more of an upland and the valley more of a valley!

As we looked for a way to follow through on this planning principle, we discovered that there were three distinct regions on our site. Together, these regions formed a subset of the upland-to-lowland planning unit, and each had its own special natural and three-dimensional qualities. The first one we called the River Reach North, where the main stem of Hyland Creek connects our site with the other adjacent neighbourhoods to the north and west. The second one we called River Reach Centre, which runs diagonally through the site and captures the bottom of the bowl and the natural centre of the site. The third we called the River Reach South, which is the gradual opening up of the south edge of the bowl towards the Serpentine River Valley.

The interesting thing about these three "reaches" of the river is that they are actually different watersheds. Each watershed is a subwatershed of Hyland Creek. Hyland Creek, in the same way, is a subwatershed of the Serpentine River. It is axiomatic: If we are to have a more sustainable urban landscape, we must start rehabilitating watersheds at all scales, from the river system scale to the neighbourhood scale – but *especially* at the neighbourhood scale. Why especially at the neighbourhood scale? Because it is the neighbourhood that pollutes the river, not the other way around.

The Valley of Two Waters
If we can start putting the pieces of the urban puzzle together, linking these watersheds in an integrated natural and spatial system (a system that allows nature to push back against the grid), then we can start to link these neighbourhood systems together! Eventually, you could have a community-wide ecological and recreational system. This system can connect our people – via walkways, bikeways, and the occasional parkway – along the threads of the streams and riverways. Since water runs downhill, this system will naturally gather the highland districts and join them together in the central river valley. In this way, Surrey may reorient its community, sustainably, towards the unifying Serpentine River and Nicomekl River plain.

So thinking about our site as just one small part of this much bigger system, we took the idea of water one step further; we took a positive stance towards the roads, drains, and service systems of the site. Given our concern for watersheds at all scales, we became particularly interested in how the road and the storm-drain infrastructure could be used in a positive and creative way. Eventually we came up with the idea of "The Valley of Two Waters." In this concept, storm-water (and, potentially, grey water) is held *up* and *over* the stream system. In most conventional storm-drain systems, water is collected in underground pipes and dumped into the nearest available stream or river, thus creating all kinds of problems for fish and fowl. Even the more advanced alternative storm-drain systems merely mitigate rather than integrate storm run-off. In our plan there are no underground pipes; in our plan, surface storm-water runoff is never released into the stream. We propose to run this water *on the surface,* down street-side swales to a redesigned 64th Avenue. Sixty-Fourth Avenue then becomes a new kind of parkway, which we have called the "Water Parkway." It is lined with artificial marshes that clean the storm run-off and grey water as it flows east to the Serpentine River. As the parkway moves towards the Serpentine River, it becomes wider, more green, more wet, and has bigger marshes and taller trees. In this way, the transportation viaduct becomes a public aqueduct!

The Water Parkway is also a point of intersection and distribution for the multi-modal transportation system. Bikeways and pathways run along, over, and under 64th Avenue to and from transportation stops. The paths lead back up the streamways through a variety of environments, up fairly steep hills and across flat plains, to connect with virtually every residential street. This system connects and expresses both the highland and the lowland realms of the site. The systems of parkways, pathways, and bikeways are also designed to provide a continuous, diverse, and uninterrupted natural habitat. In this way, the plants, animals, and birds can feel connected, just as do human beings. Since all these systems – transportation, recreation, natural habitat, and ecological protection – are integrated, they are less expensive to acquire, build and maintain. With integrated systems, the city's infrastructure budget can be pooled in order to get multiple and maximum impacts for each dollar spent.

An Integration of the Habitat Structure with the Cultural Structure
In our plan, most of the public functions are integrated with the natural and recreational systems. Since those systems come together in the centre of the site, this is where we also locate public functions. In this way, the cultural structure and the habitat structure become one integrated system.

Residential neighbourhoods surround the centre of the site. We worked at densities of about eighteen units per acre, which sounds fairly dense. But if you handle the architecture correctly, you still have enough space for everybody to have their own garden. Much higher-density mixed commercial, light industrial, and residential developments are located along the King George Highway transit way. The monumental grove of Douglas Fir, situated strategically at the curve of King George Highway, where it is visible for miles in both directions, has been preserved to focus the district. The district is transit friendly and easily accessible.

As the density on the ridge lands increases, the basic form of the site is emphasized; low-density housing is located at the bottom, merged with and subordinate to the forest, high-density housing is located at the top, creating a crown for the hill and a very important landmark for the city.

In this plan, we begin to see a very different way of organizing the city. This site focuses not on the highlands, but on the waterways down to the river valley. Civic and recreational functions are found in the lowlands, while high-density growth is found on the ridge. Waterways guide the movement of people and animals, emphasizing the basic skeleton of this "City of Parks" – the streams. This language of integration can be used on this site to great effect. More important, this language of integration can and should be used throughout the many upland-to-lowland areas yet to be developed in Surrey. If this were to be done, hundreds of millions of dollars of unnecessary expenditures would be avoided, scores of miles of recreational trails would be in place, the salmon streams would be protected, our housing would be more affordable, and the special three-dimensional qualities of the Surrey natural landscape – its very special sense of place – would be emphasized.

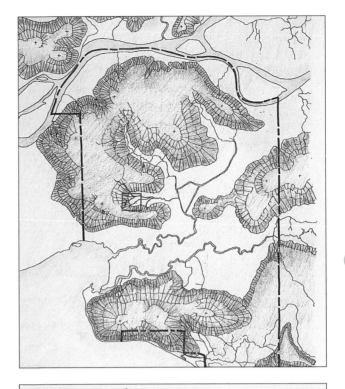

Top right:
About half of Surrey's land area is protected from urban development, as it lies within the boundaries of the Agricultural Land Reserve (shown in white). Most of the citizens of Surrey live in the brown-tinted upland areas, particularly in the highest areas (shown in light brown).

Bottom right:
The river valley area appears as an empty white area in most city planning documents; the one shown here is but one example. Interestingly, this map also shows how many "housing opportunity" areas are located at the edge of this river valley. This plan also clearly shows how extensively the river and stream system penetrates into many parts of the community.

Right:
This diagram shows how the Serpentine and Nicomekl valleys can unify the far flung neighbourhoods and recreational resources of the community. The site (shown in light brown) is a turning point and an entrance point to two powerful landscapes – the upland and the lowland of Surrey.

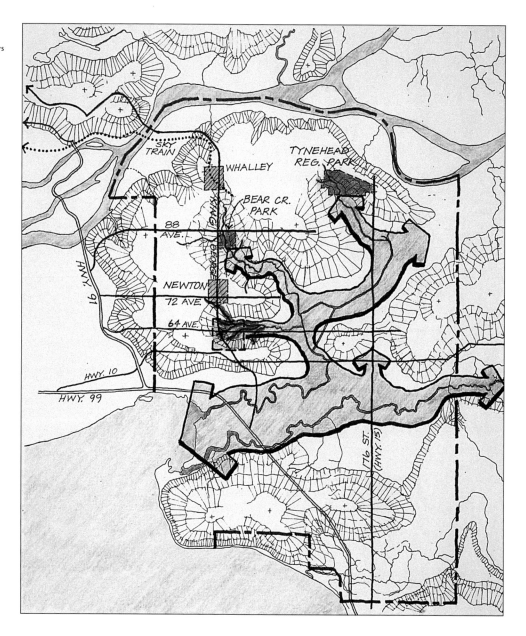

Top right:
This view to the east reveals the basic shape of the site and its relationship to the larger lowland landscape. The site includes upland, lowland, and important transitional landscapes. The study site proper is delimited by the heavy dashed black line.

Centre right:
We propose to bring the Serpentine River to the upland. In this way we can express and enhance the three-dimensional environmental qualities of the study site.

Bottom right:
We propose to run this water *on the surface,* down street-side swales to a redesigned 64th Avenue. Sixty-Fourth Avenue then becomes an ecological parkway lined with artificial marshes that clean the storm run-off and grey water as it flows to the Serpentine River. As the Water Parkway moves towards the Serpentine River, collecting more storm run-off as it goes, it becomes wider, greener, and includes ever-larger marshes. All of this urban run-off is kept out of the Hyland Creek system, ensuring that the natural streams will stay clean. The streams will still be fed by clean water from ground-water sources and by surface run-off from the conservation and recreation areas.

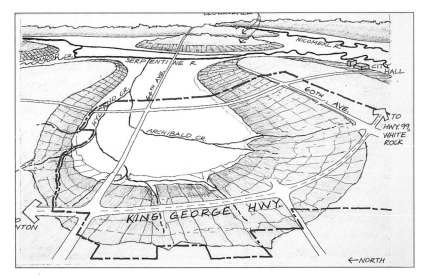

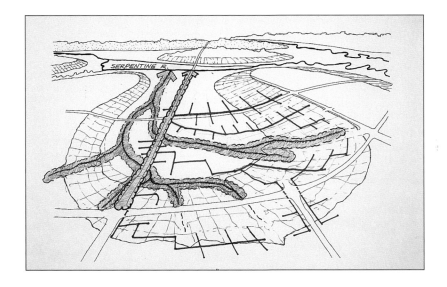

Right:

The three distinct "River Reaches" of the site. These three distinct places are a subset of the larger upland-to-lowland landscape type. Each of these reaches has its own distinct feel. Each reach is a subwatershed of the Hyland Creek watershed, which is itself a subwatershed of the Serpentine River watershed.

Far right:

Our proposal locates medium- and low-density housing in the lowland and on the slopes, high-density housing on and near the ridge. As the higher elevations are built up and the lower elevations are preserved, the basic form of the site is emphasized. Civic functions are grouped among the natural and recreational open spaces in the lowest areas of the site.

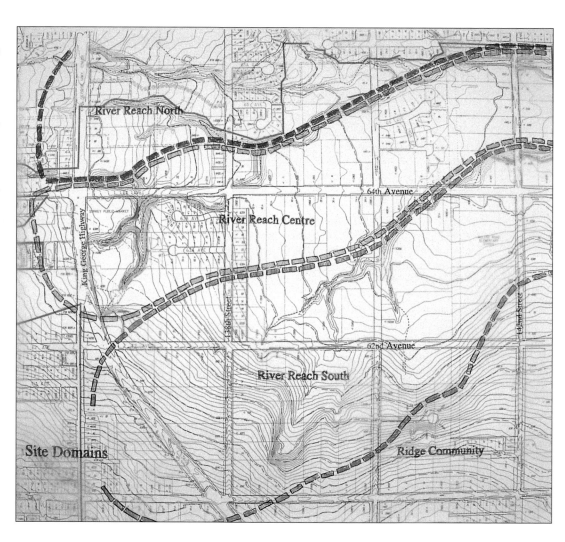

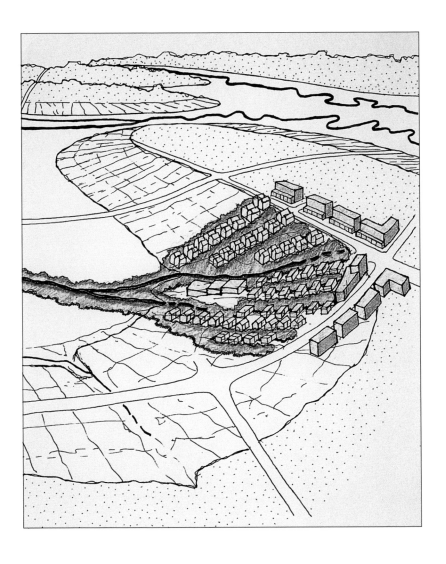

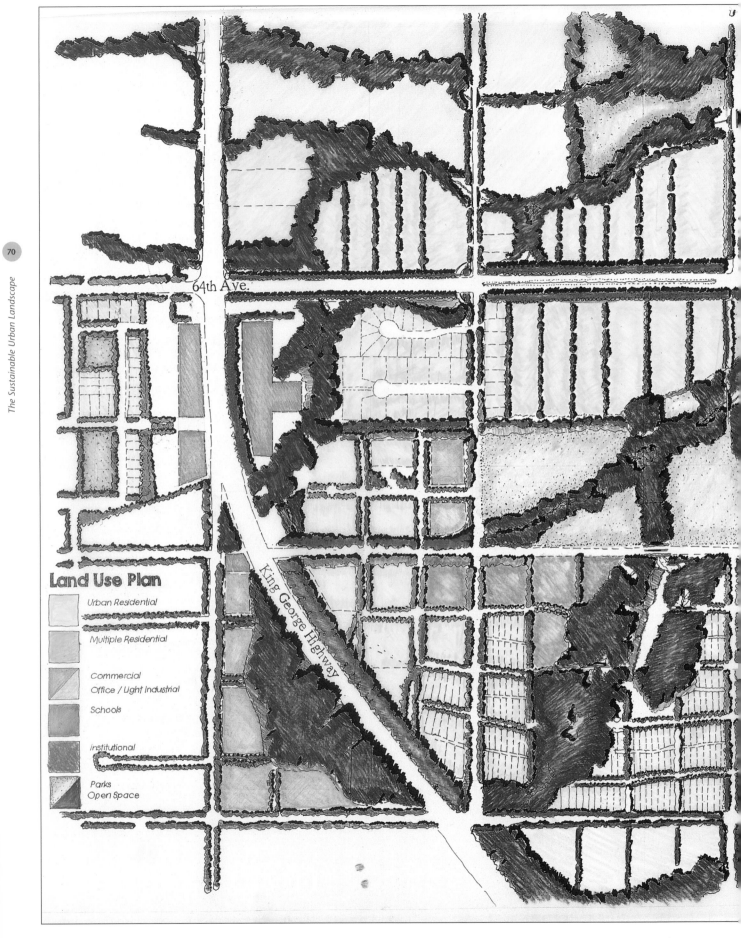

64th Ave.

King George Highway

Land Use Plan

Urban Residential

Multiple Residential

Commercial
Office / Light Industrial

Schools

Institutional

Parks
Open Space

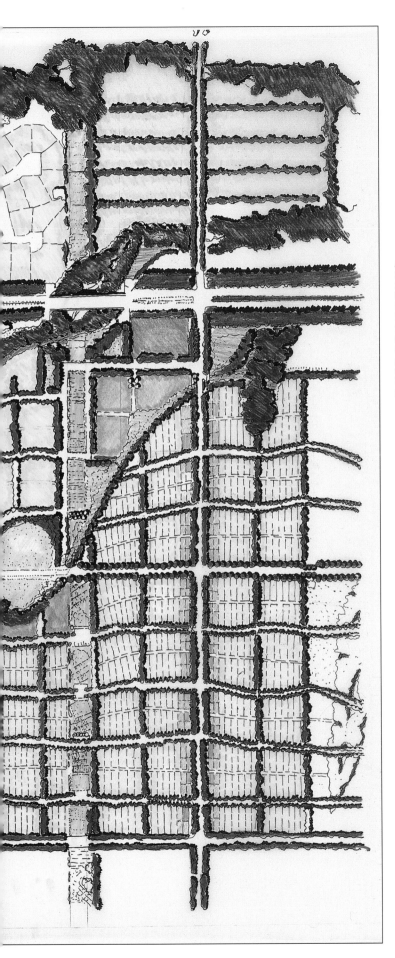

Left:
Land-use plan for the site.
Lower-density housing is shown
in yellow, higher-density
housing in orange. Commercial/
light industrial space is shown in
red. Public and civic buildings
are shown in light blue near the
centre of the site and are
grouped with the recreation and
conservation areas, shown in
light green and dark green,
respectively.

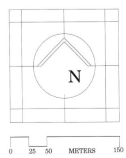

N

0   25   50   METERS   150

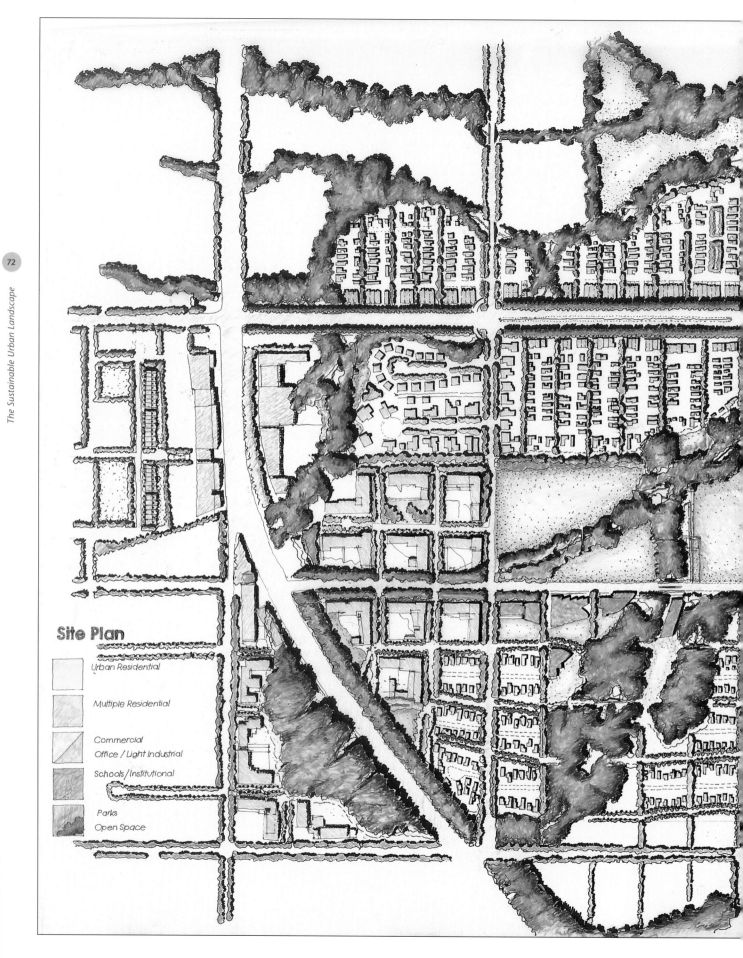

Site Plan

Urban Residential

Multiple Residential

Commercial
Office / Light Industrial

Schools / Institutional

Parks
Open Space

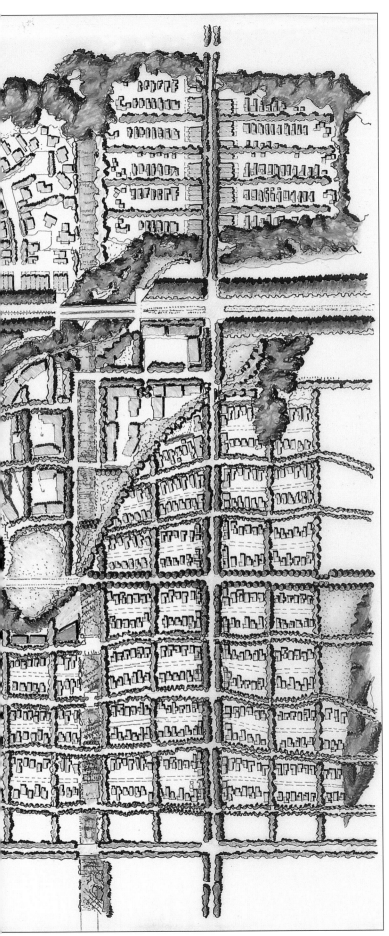

Left:

Illustrative site plan. The green fingers of the drainage system penetrate to the heart of the site and all the way to King George Highway. The important stand of Douglas Fir is shown at the curve of King George Highway. The green fingers serve as habitat and recreation corridors, linking the site to the Serpentine River Valley via the main stem of Hyland Creek. The use of the neighbourhood grid ensures that cars, bicycles, and pedestrians can always travel via the most direct route, even though traffic is dispersed. The 64th Avenue Water Parkway cuts through the northern side of the site. It gathers all of the storm run-off delivered by the roadside swales. The neighbourhood grid is warped where necessary to allow for natural and gradual water flow down the sides of streets. All neighbourhood storm-water is brought to the parkway, where it collects in channels and artificial marshes. The water moves slowly and continuously east to the Serpentine River. As more water collects, the parkway widens to sixty metres to hold this increased flow. As it widens, the parkway becomes a major recreational amenity and visual landmark for the district.

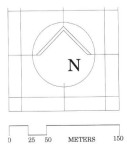

N

0   25   50   METERS   150

Right:
Three basic housing types are suggested in this proposal. The highest-density housing is located in three-storey condominium-style buildings, as shown at top right – this type is grouped in the two areas (shown in orange) on the land-use plan. The area that borders the Water Parkway is dominated by the housing type shown at middle right – here, the rear portions of existing lots are filled in with individual structures grouped as a sub-neighbourhood. The front of the lot has a band of townhouses that line the parkway. The third type, shown at the bottom right, is found on the sloping portions of the site. These are 35 by 100 foot lots, a lot size that is typical of older parts of Vancouver. Grading details on this plan explain how surface run-off would flow down street-side swales to naturalized water collection areas.

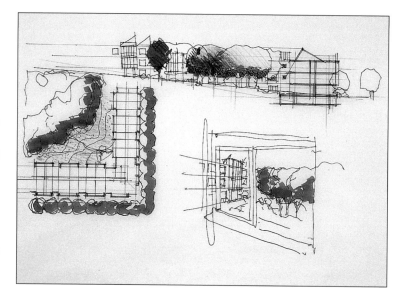

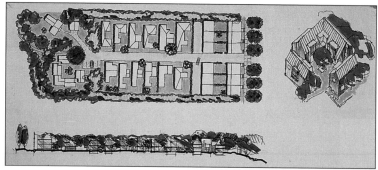

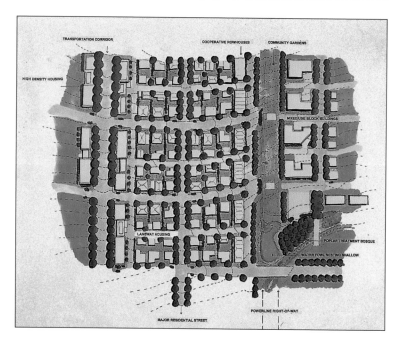

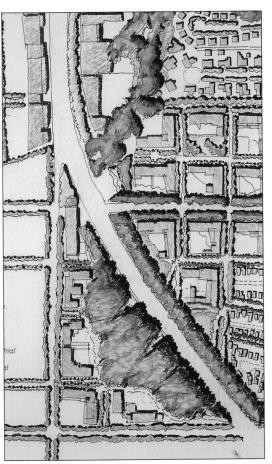

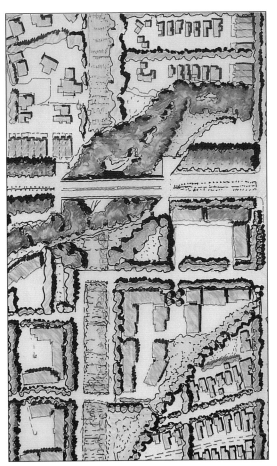

Top left:

A high density commercial and light industrial area is grouped around the landmark stand of hundred-foot tall Douglas Fir. Natural areas connect this stand – visually, as habitat, and as a pedestrian walkway – to the larger natural and recreational system of the site.

Top right:

This detail shows a major point of intersection between the natural and cultural realms. Archibald Creek and its attendant recreational trails flow under the Water Parkway. The Water Parkway bridges the creek to allow for easy migration of fish, animals, and people. Roadside bikeway and footpath systems intersect with stream-side systems at this important intersection. Neighbourhood commercial areas and a transit stop provide additional activity at this important node.

Bottom:

The schools, library, community facilities, and public offices are arranged along 62nd Avenue amid the major natural and recreational areas of the site. Playing fields, via naturalized meadows at their edges, are blended with forests. All of the river corridors contain walking and biking paths.

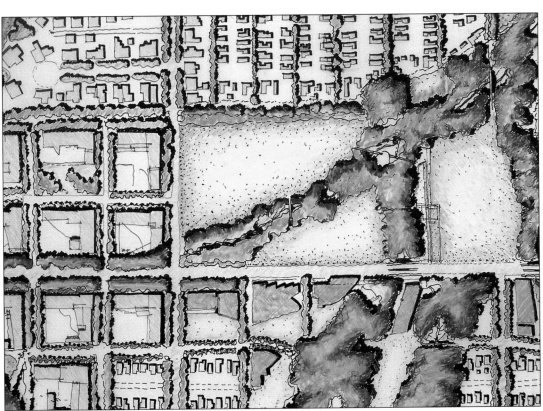

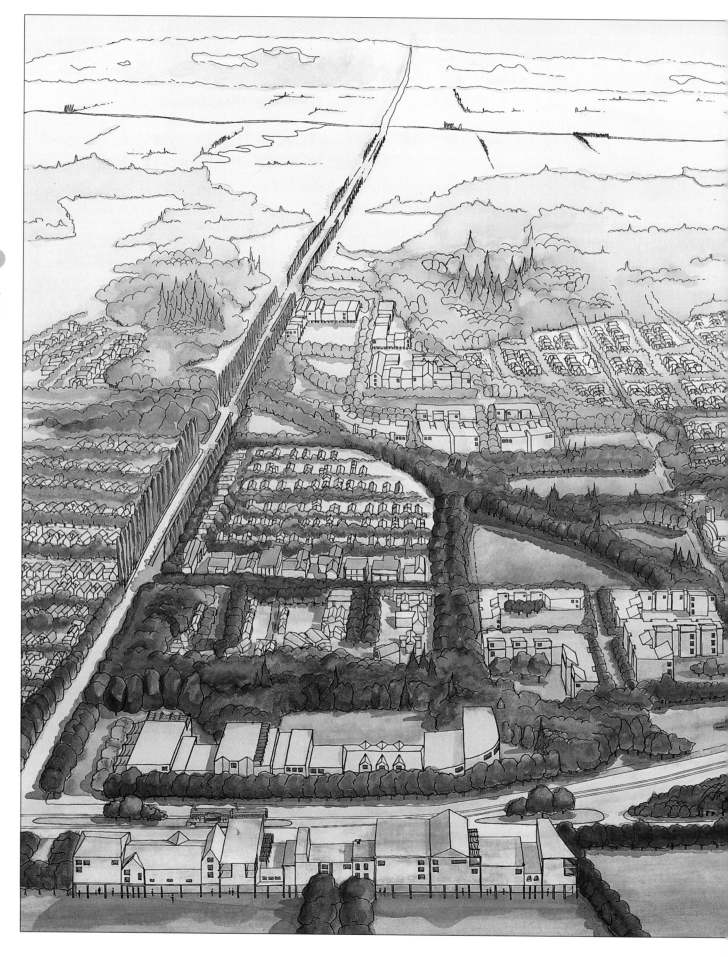

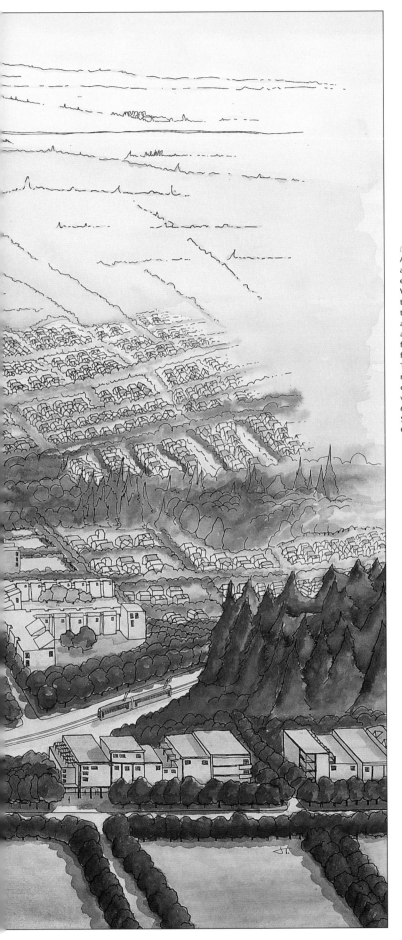

Left:
Aerial perspective view of the area as proposed. View is to the east, with the Serpentine River Valley in the middleground and the upland area of Cloverdale in the distance. The Hyland Creek and Archibald Creek system are clearly visible as the dark forested bands that merge and flow to the Serpentine River. The 64th Avenue Water Parkway moves from the lower left-hand corner to the top centre of the view. The importance of the 64th Avenue link across the Serpentine River Valley to Cloverdale is obvious.

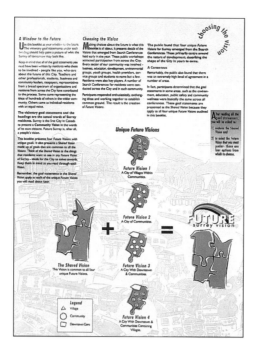

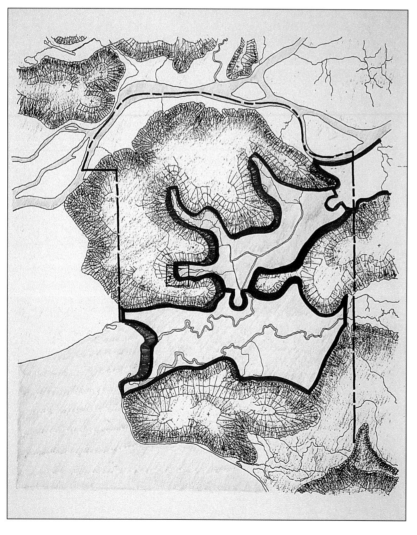

Left and below:
The Surrey "Future Vision" planning process uses the metaphor of the puzzle piece as a way to suggest an urban design vision for the city. But the pieces of the urban design puzzle are not to be found in abstractions like "community," "village," and "downtown." Surrey's three-dimensional natural environments, and, in particular, its major and minor watersheds, are the real puzzle pieces. When the pieces of the puzzle are put together, the centre of the puzzle is clearly located in the Serpentine River Valley and the Nicomekl River Valley, while the edges of each piece locate areas of crucial urban design importance.

BEAUTIFUL INFRASTRUCTURE

By the Design Center
for American Urban Landscape

WILLIAM R MORRISH
Principal Investigator

Several years ago, Minnesota citizens voted to establish the Legislative Commission on Minnesota Resources (LCMR), a trust which reserves a portion of state lottery revenues to fund environmental projects. The Commission recommended a proposal submitted by the University of Minnesota's Design Center for American Urban Landscape to appropriate lottery funds to develop urban design principles. The principals help infrastructure projects respond to the typical concerns now facing many local communities. As communities mature, the cultural character and ecologies of place seem to disappear. Instead, regional nuances give way to a cluttered and confusing landscape of homogenized commercial and residential developments and the growing anonymity of the metropolitan environment.

The urban design ideas for "Beautiful Infrastructure" are illustrated with sites located around the Minneapolis-St. Paul Metropolitan region. Many of the examples are from urban areas. Two of the more rural sites are in high-growth areas that are slated for infrastructural development: a highway upgrade in rural Chanhassen; and new development at the edge of rural lands in the agricultural town of Farmington.

Beautiful infrastructure, which responds to the physical and topographical features of the locale, is primary to creating community identity and a personal sense of orientation. Unfortunately, infrastructure is often regarded as a neutral grey utility devoid of cultural expression or celebration. While vital and costly capital-infrastructure projects increasingly dominate the budget agendas and physical environments of local communities, too often their potential as multifunctional systems has been overlooked. Infrastructure shows its full complexity only when viewed with both the lens of an ecologist, who sees the interrelationships within natural systems, and the lens of the urban designer, who sees the features and patterns that enrich people's experience within the landscape.

About Terminology

Until now, we've associated infrastructure with industry and national defense. As a result, the terms for its planning and design are technical and standardized. We need a more precise language which integrates both ecological function and urban design. To enlarge functional engineering terms to include infrastructure's ecological, cultural and social layers, we draw upon the terminology of landscape ecology and environmental design. Landscape ecology includes human activities as part of the environment and focuses on spatial forms in ecological systems, such as corridors, networks, edges and patches. Environmental designers such as Kevin Lynch also created a vocabulary for the landscape that included terms such as rooms, neighborhoods, districts, landmarks and paths. In naming a place, we can use language to transform our understanding of systems and places. For example the words prairie waterway instead of storm-water drainage ditch describe a series of proposed community stream corridors.

Enriching Sense of Place:
Outdoor "Rooms" in the Landscape

Natural features, as well as infrastructure such as highways, bridges and storm sewers, can create or restore community identity. These systems define the public realm, accentuating its unique spatial organization and delineating outdoor "rooms" in the landscape.

In rural Chanhassen, there are a variety of rooms, formed by its rolling hills, sky lines, built structures and infrastructure systems The resulting composition is a mixture of urban and rural rooms. A proposed upgrade to the highway through Chanhassen offers opportunities to create new rooms and enhance existing ones. In addition,

First published in *On The Ground; The Multimedia Journal on Community, Design & Environment*. Vol. 1, No. 2, Winter/Spring 1995. Reprinted with permission.

pedestrian and vehicle links that have similar design elements on both sides of the highway create rooms that bridge the highway corridor. Different types of rooms experienced in a sequence along the highway give the sense that the road is passing through specific places, rather than along an anonymous strip development. Diagram 1 shows different types of landscape rooms, including transit rooms, landmark intersections, civic spaces, and commercial nodes, along the highway corridor.

Bridging the Community with Corridors, Networks and Landmarks

Many connections amongst the Mississippi River and areas in the Twin Cities region offer a wide variety of recreational and environmental opportunities. The terms "recreational" and "environmental" are used in the broadest, most inclusive sense. The daily commuter, migrating wildlife and leisure bicyclists are all potential users of different kinds of river connections. In addition, these connections also serve an array of commercial services, work sites, and residential areas.

Corridors:
Sharing the Community Life Lines

"Corridors" are linear spaces that accommodate movement or visual access, like a hallway in a house that provides access to a series of rooms along its length. Corridors may work as a permeable boundary between places or as a conduit to local landmarks. Diagram 2 shows a range of corridor types for a hypothetical River Community. Roadways as corridors, for example, are more than just single-use, functional rights-of-way defined by curbs. Roadways can be great, linear hallways with permeable walls shaped by the natural and built features along the road. Often passers-by assess a place by the character of its roadway; people use roadway features to orient themselves. Corridors become

richly layered cultural and environmental spaces which help define and connect sectors of the community. The proposed highway upgrade in Chanhassen offers an opportunity to create rooms off its hallway as shown in Diagram 3.

Networks:
Creating a Hierarchical Web of Movement

Networks are webs of alternative routes that offer tertiary systems of movement apart from major roadways. Networks connect the destinations of home, work and marketplaces to the community's environmental and cultural resources. Hubs along a network are places where trails, roads, paths and natural systems intersect, often made distinctive by landmarks or other cultural or natural features. Diagram 4 shows network types for a hypothetical river community.

Enhancing Ecological Function

New development has added more impervious surfaces to the landscape, such as roads, roofs, parking lots and turf (whose storm-water absorbency rate equals that of concrete). These hard surfaces repel, rather than absorb, rain, increasing the amount of storm water pouring into piped drainage ways, such as storm sewers. These efficient conduits quickly funnel valuable topsoil and pollutants, such as roadway runoff and lawn fertilizers, into lakes and streams. As underground aquifers are depleted, causing some lakes and streams to dry up, major rivers ironically swell beyond capacity. Land that is left undeveloped is often a fragmented scattering of natural habitat resource islands.

Knowing where water originates and where it flows is essential to making decisions about land uses that will reconnect the community's natural resources and protect property values. The unique identity of the community watershed dictates environmentally sound patterns of development

that vary from one site to another. A variety of watershed types in a hypothetical river community is shown in Diagram 5.

Instead of piping storm water as quickly as possible into rivers and lakes, we should explore alternatives that introduce more complexity to these systems. Exposed drainage ways, for example, provide space for plants that filter and recharge water. Strategies that rely on ecological features and functions of the landscape do require more land and therefore additional property costs. These costs may be minor compared to the initial and long-term municipal maintenance costs of concrete-and-steel systems. In addition, neighborhoods bordering a protected green corridor command higher property values. Even if drainage ways aren't exposed, the piped rights-of-way can be wide enough to accommodate pathways planted with native species, thus enhancing the value of adjoining properties.

Watersheds and Habitat:
Making a Home for All

Complex systems may also be more economical in the long term. They're multi-use, providing twice the benefit for a single investment. Farmington's prairie waterway system was designed not only to provide recreational and wildlife connections to the Vermillion River, but also to purify storm water and surface water runoff. Cleaning these waters at the source is important because improving the quality of the water flowing into major rivers and lakes may eliminate the need for building costly treatment facilities later. The Prairie Waterway design complexity is shown in Diagram 6.

Most parks are typically planted with turf and randomly spaced trees. This monoculture of grass, in addition to sparse tree canopies, cannot sustain the diverse plant communities that support many species of wildlife. Groves of native trees, however, create patches of woodland habitat. Large tracts not only provide habitat for forest species but also may frame views and form outdoor rooms. Obsolete land uses or derelict lands also offer opportunities to restore natural systems. Planted with native vegetation, linear waterways also serve as habitat corridors in the metropolitan area. These wet environments provide nesting, resting and foraging sites for a variety of wildlife. Cross-sections of the plantings for the prairie water way are shown in Diagrams 7a and 7b.

Conclusion

To build infrastructure that participates deeply in the imaginative life of its community requires a fundamental shift in our attitude toward landscape. In his book *Discovering the Vernacular Landscape*, John Brinckerhoff Jackson, the noted scholar on American landscape, says that "the most magnificent of city complexes" recognized the need to integrate infrastructure, or civil engineering, with landscape, or architecture. Beautiful and brilliant schemes are created when "they both reorganize space for human needs, both produce works of art in the truest sense."

For Jackson, Infrastructure not only provides the backdrop for culture but the very ingredients that make it possible:
In the contemporary world it is by recognizing this similarity of purpose that we will eventually formulate a new definition of landscape; a composition of man-made or man-modified spaces to serve as infrastructure or background for our collective existence; and if background seems inappropriately modest we should remember that in our modern use of the word it means that which underscores not only our identity and presence, but also our history.

J.B. Jackson's definition of landscape sets forth a challenge to the standard infrastructure mission statement to supply goods, services and people to their proper destinations. His definition of landscape relies on the necessity for elements of infrastructure

to fulfil broader cultural, social and ecological functions to become part of the supportive infrastructure or background for our "collective existence, identity and presence, and history." We believe that this composite "man-made or man-modified" landscape is created by infrastructure that enriches our sense of place, bridges our commonwealth and enhances ecological function.

Design Center for American Urban Landscape team:

William R. Morrish,
    Dayton Hudson Professor in Urban Design, Director and Principal Investigator
Catherine R. Brown,
    Dayton Hudson Senior Fellow in Urban Design and Coordinator of Special Projects
Regina E Bosignore,
    Landscape Architecture
Andrew Comfort,
    Architecture
Adelheid Fischer,
    Writer
M. Elizabeth Fitzsimmons,
    Landscape Architecture
Thomas Hammerberg,
    Landscape Architecture
Betsy Leverty,
    Finance
Daniel J. Marskel,
    Architecture
Ross Martin,
    Landscape Architecture
R.G. Schunn,
    Architecture
Carol Swenson,
    Geography
Mary Vogel,
    Architecture

Professional Advisors to Project Team

Janine Benyus,
    Natural Resource Science Writer
Harrison Fraser,
    Dean of the College of Architecture and Landscape Architecture, University of Minnesota
Eugene A. Hickok,
    JMM Consulting Engineers, Inc.
Steve Johnson,
    River Management Coordinator MN Department of Natural Resources, Division of Waters
Joan Nassauer,
    Head, Department of Landscape Architecture, University of Minnesota
Jack Mauritz,
    Consultant, Environmental/Recreational Planning
Robert McMaster,
    Associate Professor, Department of Geography, University of Minnesota
Ian McHarg,
    Professor Emeritus, University of Pennsylvania
Lance M. Neckar,
    Associate Professor, Department of Landscape Architecture, University of Minnesota
Daniel Parks,
    JMM Consulting Engineers Inc.
Leslie Sauer,
    Principal, Andropogon Associates, Ltd.

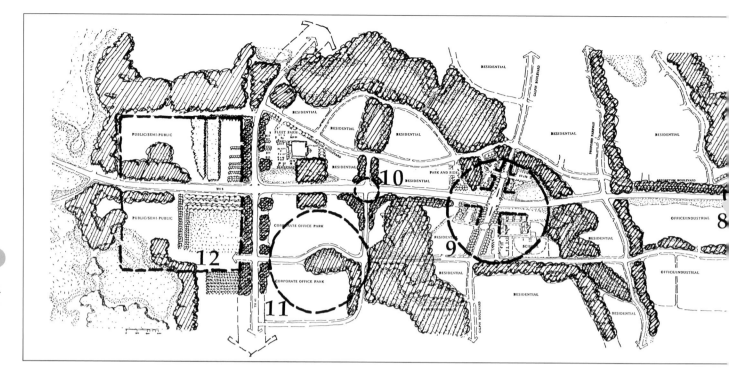

Above:

DIAGRAM 1

LANDSCAPE ROOMS

1
Transit entrance: introduces landscape qualities that will be carried through the corridor, including park and ride lots with shaded and wind-protected environments.

2
Landmark intersections: sculpted to mark gateway to main street.

3
Service room: convenience facilities edged by windbreak vegetation and street trees.

4
Downtown: boulevard continued, fronted by commercial retail, service and civic spaces.

5
Wetland Circle: ponds with edges defined with wetland and aquatic plant materials.

6
Long view room: vantage point to preview the landscape ahead; signals the edge of downtown.

7
Lake Ann room: a civic park space enclosed by drainage ways, forests and windbreak vegetation, extending to include the business park south of Highway 5

8
Western entrance to Lake Ann: a park entrance room for future residents and employees.

9
Community commercial center: uses the stream corridor windbreak vegetation and buildings to build a service node "neighborhood niche" convenient to home, school and work.

10
Upper Bluff Creek intersection: a formally planted entry way with all corners relating to each other.

11
Arboretum Gateway Office Park: centered around a formal wetland planting.

12
Arboretum Gateway: formal, agricultural planted entrance, to include Highway 41 as an edge, complimenting the plantings of the office park. Together the planted edges make the lake to river gateway.

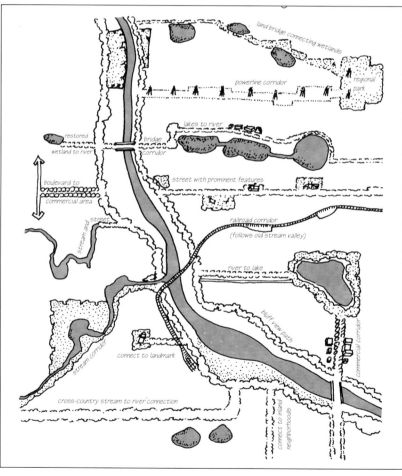

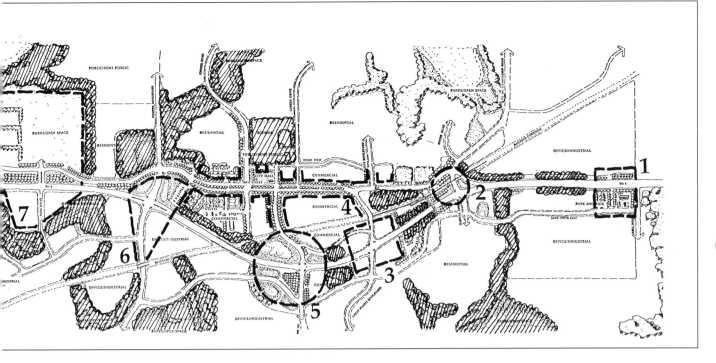

Left:
DIAGRAM 2
CORRIDOR TYPES
This diagram catalogues some of
the many types of corridors that
can connect an urban river
landscape. Corridors can vary in
character and serve multiple
functions. Existing linear
features may signal corridors
that can be targeted for
environmental and recreational
enhancements.

Right:
DIAGRAM 3
HIGHWAY CORRIDORS
The upper diagram shows a
typical highway corridor with
strip development along the
highway; the lower diagram
shows proposed highway rooms
and corridor using local
landscape features along with
the environmental systems to
enhance a sense of community
across the highway.

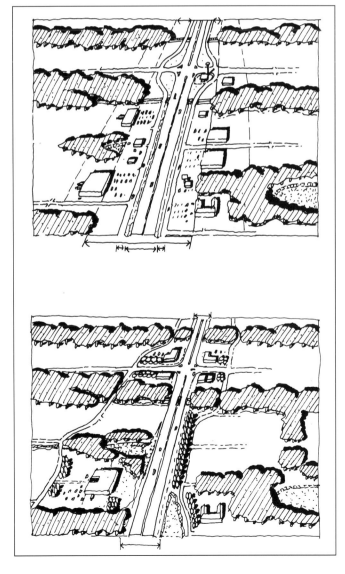

DIAGRAM 4
NETWORK TYPES
This diagram highlights the types of existing resources that can form a river network of hubs, landmarks, spokes and loops, symbolized in dashed lines. The scale and character of these movement systems can be as varied as the communities that make up the river landscape.

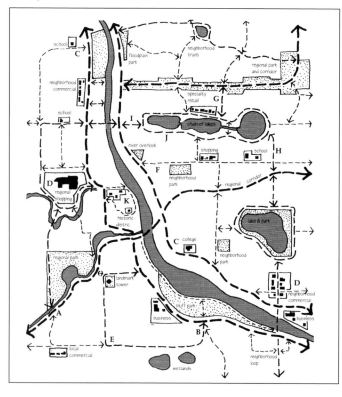

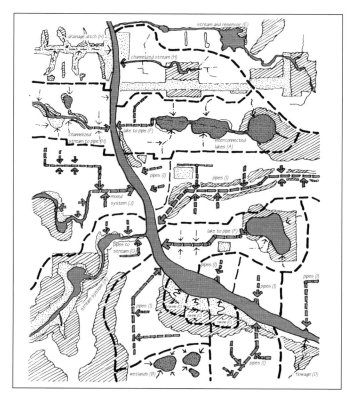

Above:
DIAGRAM 5
WATERSHED TYPES
Traditionally engineered drainage systems are shown above as dashed lines with arrows. These networks have typically superseded natural channels and basins, with a reduction of wildlife habitat. High environmental and municipal costs for traditional structural systems have spurred the search for new approaches to flood control and water-quality protection, including limiting development on flood plains and creating new wetland areas where additional capacity and filtration is needed. Cross hatched sections represent wooded habitat; wetlands and grasslands are shaded.

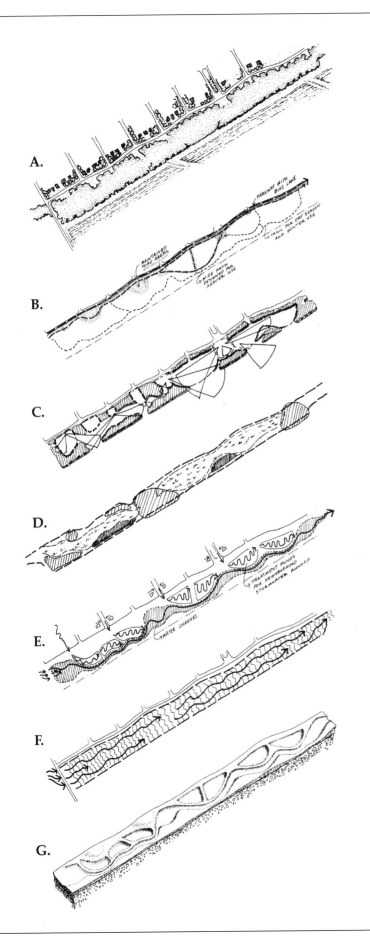

A.

B.

C.

D.

E.

F.

G.

Left:
DIAGRAM 6
ELEMENTS OF THE PRAIRIE WATERWAY

A
City's Edge: The prairie waterway creates a transition between city and country, a permeable edge between the two land uses. Sheltering trees provide a vantage point from which to view the open croplands to the east. Views from the open country to town are defined by a horizon of vegetation.

B
Community Recreation: Seasonal changes of vegetation and wildlife can be observed from the parkway drive and community streets, which link pedestrians to the creek channel. The parkway drive and bicycle lanes gently meander to provide changing views of the waterway and the countryside. A broad path is paved to accommodate all-weather use. A low-maintenance trail, usable for winter and dry season walks, weaves through the prairie and lowland forest landscape. Turf areas, maintained for active play and picnic areas, are located at the ends of city streets.

C
Rooms and Views: Tree masses, water-cleaning ponds and low embankments define outdoor rooms and views. A variety of experiences unfold as park users move along the water corridor. Small rooms and intricate views give way to longer, wider rooms and more expansive views of the waterway and adjoining farm fields.

D
Wildlife Habitat Corridor: The linear waterway and its vegetation also serves as a habitat corridor. Planted primarily with areas of prairie grass and lowland forest, this wet environment affords movement, nesting and foraging opportunities for a variety of wildlife. The patches of deciduous and evergreen woodlands that punctuate the corridor provide shelter and food for overwintering species, such as chickadees, nuthatches and cardinals. Because this corridor links to the Vermillion River, it forms a vital connection to the region's wildlife habitat network, especially as the watershed becomes more urbanized.

E
Surface Water: The prairie waterway incorporates a water-filtration system to help clean water flowing into the Vermillion River. Chemicals, fertilizers, and salt carried by runoff from neighborhood lawns and streets first flows into ponding areas for sediment and chemical filtration. The cleaner water then joins a channel carrying water from the south end of Farmington to the Vermillion River.

F
Flood Plain: The waterway serves as storage for excess water during major rainfalls, providing holding areas for surface water as well as groundwater pushed to the surface.

G
Topography: Low embankments separate channel and ponding areas. These earthworks are relatively shallow and do not penetrate a groundwater-filled layer of gravel just below the topsoil.

WOODLAND CROSS-SECTION

CURVILINEAR PARKWAY AND JOGGING PATH | SILVER MAPLES | FARMINGTON CREEK CHANNEL | WHITE SPRUCE GROVE | HIGHBUSH CRANBERRY HEDGE

Elevation 896.5
Elevation 896.0
Existing gra
High water table level 892
Low water table level 890
High water table
Low water table

OPEN MEADOW CROSS-SECTION

STREET TREES | TREATMENT PONDS | FARMINGTON CREEK CHANNEL | COTTONWOOD GROVE | SCOTCH PINE WINDBREAK

High water table el. 891
Low water table el. 889
High water table el. 891
Low water table el. 889

Above and right:
DIAGRAM 7A
PRAIRE WATERWAY CROSS SECTIONS
DIAGRAM 7B
PRAIRIE WATERWAY PLAN
Woodland Cross-Section, shown above and located on plan at right. The curvilinear parkway and jogging path is planted with hardwoods, such as swamp white oak, a relatively fast-growing lowland oak with a generous canopy for shade.

Silver Maples, fast-growing lowland trees with a very wide canopy, enclose lawn openings for active play and picnics.

The Farmington Creek Channel, approximately 40 feet wide including side slopes, is planted with water-tolerant prairie grasses and wetland plants. Red twig dogwoods help stabilize the bank and provide low shrub cover for wildlife.

White Spruce groves, lowland forest conifers, are large enough to provide winter cover and habitat for small mammals and songbirds such as cardinals. An all-season pedestran trail winds through the evergreen trees.

Highbush Cranberry is a source of food and shelter for wildlife. The hedge adds a middle habitat layer to the lowland forest vegetation.

Estimates of the high water table and low water table, illustrated in the shaded layer shown below the soil surface, are based on data from the City of Farmington and the Dakota County Soil Survey.

Open Meadow Cross-Section, also shown above and located on plan at right. Street trees are selected for their tolerance for salt and wet soil conditions, such as hackberry, swamp white oak and ash.

Treatment ponds are planted with wetland and wet prairie vegetation to filter neighbour-hood runoff.

The Farmington Creek Channel, approximately 40 feet wide including side slopes, is planted with water-tolerant prairie grasses and wetland plants. Unlike the sense of enclosure created by trees in the woodland design, the openness of the prairie meadow landscape gives this waterway section a more expansive feel.

Cottonwood groves, mass plantings of fast-growing lowland trees, provide a wide canopy and protective cover for wildlife.

Scotch Pine windbreaks cut the force of the winter winds and provide habitat for songbirds and small mammals. At the same time, the windbreak defines an edge between the agricultural fields to the east and the community to the west.

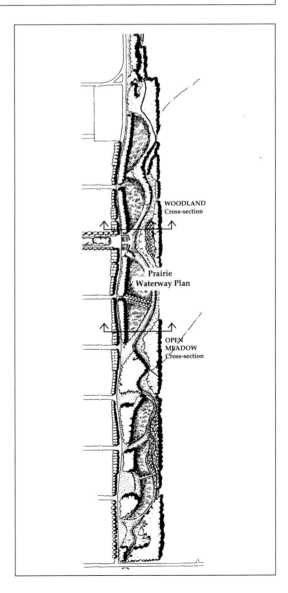

WOODLAND Cross-section

Prairie Waterway Plan

OPEN MEADOW Cross-section

APPENDICES

Design Performance Criteria

The Design Brief

Design Charrette Advisory Board

Design Charrette Team Leaders

DESIGN PERFORMANCE CRITERIA

The Charrette Project Plan

In their assessment of the state of the global biosphere, the World Commission on Environment and Development concludes that many solutions to global environmental problems will be found at the site and community level of development. The UBC Chair in Landscape and Liveable Environments, the major sponsor for the Charrette Project, focuses on developing design responses that would make our sites and communities more sustainable.

Between September of 1995 and September of 1998 we intend to advance the objectives of the Chair by conducting a series of design charrettes. These charrettes are week-long design projects where leading designers from our region and from around the world will work together intensively to illustrate practical solutions to the problems of site and community sustainability. Three charrettes are planned. Each charrette will test the same general principles of sustainability; but the three sites will have different contexts. This first charrette will test a site that is not yet urbanized; the second will test a highly urban "centre city" site; the third will test a medium density site in a first ring suburb.

Goal and Objectives of the Sustainable Urban Landscapes Design Charrettes:
Goal:
To demonstrate what neighbourhoods and communities could be like if they were designed and built in conformance with emerging local, provincial and federal policies for sustainable development.

Objectives:
1. Produce sustainable community design models for real British Columbia urban landscapes.
2. Illustrate the design consequences of meeting disparate and often contradictory sustainability policy objectives.
3. Illuminate the connection between sus-

tainability and livability.
4. Show how sustainable design objectives are influenced and/or impeded by typical community subdivision and site and traffic engineering regulations.
5. Create a setting where leading British Columbian designers can exchange ideas and viewpoints with outside experts in the field of sustainable design.
6. Produce design proposals that may provide patterns and prototypes for other Georgia Basin communities.
7. Broadly disseminate the results of the charrette through a variety of means and venues—to citizens, elected representatives, policy makers, and designers – and thereby influence future public policy and legislative initiatives.

Performance Criteria for the 1995 Sustainable Urban Landscapes Design Charrette:
The emerging local, provincial and federal policies for sustainable development provide the basis for the following performance criteria. Major sources used by the charrette organizers to arrive at these performance criteria include: The British Columbia Energy Council, *Planning Today for Tomorrow's Energy. An Energy Strategy for British Columbia* (BCEC); BC Hydro, *Bringing Electricity to the Livable Region* (BCH); The City of Vancouver, *Clouds of Change, Final Report of the City of Vancouver Task Force on Atmospheric Change* (CV); The Commission on Resources and Environment: *Finding Common Ground: A Shared Vision for Land Use in British Columbia* (CORE); The Province of British Columbia: *Municipal Act Section 942 and Section 945 (Growth Management Legislation)* (MA); The Greater Vancouver Regional District: *Livable Region Strategy: Proposals* (LRS); BC Transit, *Transit and Land Use Planning* (BCT); City of Surrey, *City of Surrey Official Community Plan Background Report*

No. 1; Surrey; Existing Policies (CS). These reports and regulations are available for each team's reference.

Policy directives included in these reports that have an obvious impact on site and community design have been converted into design performance criteria and are listed below in three categories: land and water; the built environment, and energy use. These criteria all support the goal of more sustainable neighbourhoods and communities; however, they are often contradictory when applied. For example, increasing housing density may negatively affect ground and surface water quality. These performance criteria should provide designers with a basic framework for design. Participants are encouraged to interpret and expand on these policies via the production of a specific design for the site. Each team's design for the *site* must reflect a clear vision for the *district* within the larger plan for the future of the City of Surrey.

The Land and Water

The goal of British Columbian and Canadian public policy is to protect the ecological integrity of our land and rivers, both for their intrinsic value and for their value to present and future citizens. The charrette organizers assume that urban development that protects the ecological integrity of the land and water must start "from the ground up." The ecological health of the region is dependent on the ecological health of the sites that make up the region. For example, degraded storm water (non point source pollution) shipped "off sites" into streams and tributaries is the major threat to the health of Georgia Basin salmon streams. The rivers and streams that empty into the Georgia Basin comprise the world's most important salmon producing system. Extraordinary efforts are required to protect this habitat. The charrette site includes active salmon spawning streams, tributaries to the Serpentine River to the south. For this and other reasons the site can be considered very sensitive to development. Figuring out where, how to, and how much to develop the site is consequently the greatest challenge.

1. *Environmental Protection*
   Protect and enhance all environmentally sensitive and/or degraded areas (wetlands, watercourses, ravines, watersheds, ground water recharge areas, critical wildlife habitat areas, areas with fragile or unstable soils) maintaining and/or enhancing the ecological performance of native habitats, hydrology, and landforms.[1]

2. *Open Space Linkage*
   Preserve, create, and link urban and rural open space, including parks and recreation areas. Maintain and enhance public access to streams, where environmentally sustainable.[2]

3. *Open Space Quality*
   Identify and enhance special recreation opportunities within the site, i.e. streams, topographic features, natural areas etc.[3]

4. *Sanitary Systems*
   Consider the integration of district sewage treatment and sewage treatment marshes.[4]

The Built Environment

The goal of British Columbian and Canadian public policy is to provide adequate, affordable, and appropriate housing for all citizens.

A more sustainable site and community design must integrate, not segregate land uses, income groups, and family types. Services and jobs must be located near homes and transit. Charrette participants are challenged to develop a plan that integrates and locates these various land uses.

The dominance of the automobile in our new urban landscapes must be significantly reduced. Destinations must be close and convenient before walking and biking can be viable alternative to the car. Charrette participants must produce designs that will connect people with their destinations so that the car is not the only option.

1. *Housing Equity*
   Provide a balance of housing types that meet the needs of a range of ages and lifestyles and are affordable to groups and individuals within a wide range of incomes. At least 20 percent (minimum of 720 units if 10,000 persons inhabit the site) of the housing shall be for persons with family incomes in the bottom third. Income statistics for Surrey residents are listed in the appendix, as are examples of market and subsidized housing types which are normally provided for this sector.[5]

2. *Special Needs Housing*
   Provide adequate special needs housing (seniors, disabled, family crisis victims etc., Surrey demographic information is in appendix).[6]

3. *Safety*
   Employ proven methods of enhancing community safety and sociability.[7]

4. *Jobs*
   Provide work space in commercial, office, or light industrial facilities for the working population at a rate of one job for every dwelling unit. We are assuming 350 work spaces will be required for each 1,000 residents.[8]

5. *Integration of Land Uses*
   Create a mix of building and land uses, integrating residences, work, shopping, and services (community, professional, commercial and institutional).[9]

6. *Access to Transit*
   Ensure that most persons live and work close to transit and services to reduce dependence on the automobile, promote pedestrian activity, and bicycle use.[10]

Energy Use

The goal of British Columbian and Canadian public policy is to reduce energy consumption and the pollution that this consumption causes, even while population continues to increase. Any progress toward a more sustainable future will requires large per capita reductions in the amount of energy required for building conditioning and transportation. Many of the gains to be made in this area lie in the realm of improved building technologies and improved vehicle efficiencies, and are thus outside the scope of this site and community design demonstration project; however, certain site and community design factors can powerfully affect the amount of energy required for building conditioning and transportation.

District heating can be practical at certain densities and site configurations. Solar access for winter warmth is significant in our region, where the coldest winter days tend also to be the sunniest. West facing dwelling units (with the large expanses of glass common in our region) require summer air conditioning – even though our summers are quite cool. Urban forests can significantly influence energy use. Charrette participants are challenged to design the site with due regard for climatic imperatives.

Integrating land uses and accommodating pedestrians and bicycles saves energy. Designers should show how pedestrians and bicycles are accommodated and how destinations are located within walking distance of services, transit, and jobs.

1. *Solar Heat*
   Reduce building energy requirements by providing optimal solar orientation, solar access, passive solar heating, and day-lighting.[11]

2. *Energy Infrastructure*
   Aim for the efficient use of utility infrastructure by considering utility system design as part of the community design. Consider the possibility of natural on

site sewage treatment.[12]

3. *Alternative Energy*
Provide as appropriate, or maintain flexibility to provide in the future, energy service from alternative technologies such as community scale generating systems, district heating and co-generation.[13]

4. *Design with Climate*
Enhance community microclimate through design response to wind, sun, vegetation and precipitation.[14]

5. *Auto Trip Reduction*
Reduce number and length of commuter and daily use automobile trips.[15]

6. *Auto Alternatives*
Provide safe, comfortable, barrier-free and direct pedestrian access to transit route. Provide a multi modal community route system that gives walking and biking priority over auto travel.[16]

Notes

1 CORE pgs. 14–18; MA 942.11; CS pg. 1O, 28.

2 MA 942.11(II); LRS pg. 43; CORE pg. 14, 17.

3 CORE pg. 18; CS pgs. 10, 13.

4 CORE pg. 17; MA 942.11(d); LRS pg. 42; CS pg. 10.

5 LRS pg. 45; CS pg. 31; CORE pg. 15; MA 942.11; BCEC App. pg. 1; CS pgs. 8, 2.

6 MA 942.11 (h), 945; CORE pg. 15.

7 CORE pg. 14; BCT pg. 13; CS pg. 19.

8 City of Surrey Planning Dept.; CV 46.

9 LRS pg. 44; CV pg. 46; BCH pg. 47; BCT pg. 10; BCEC App. pg. 1.

10 CORE pg. 14; LRS pg. 44; MA 942.11 (b); BCT pg. 6, 11; CV pg. 46; CS pg. 16, 31: BCH pg. 47; BCT pg. 6.

11 BCH pg. 46; MA 942.11 (m); CORE pg. 14, 16; BCEC App. pg. 2.

12 BCH pg. 46; BCEC App. pg. 2; CORE pg. 17; MA 942.11 (m).

13 BCEC App. pg. 5; BCH pg. 17; MA 942.11 (m).

14 BCH pg. 46; CORE pg. 16.

15 MA 942.11 (b); CORE pgs. 14, 16; LRS pgs. 43, 44; BCT pg. 3; BCEC App. pg. 2; CV pgs. 36, 46.

16 LRS pg. 43; CORE pg. 16; CV pgs. 34, 46; BCEC App. pg. 3; MA 942.11 (b), BCT pg. 13; CS pg. 16.

Bibliography

Initials that introduce each reference correspond to initials in footnotes above.

BCEC
Planning Today for Tomorrow's Energy: An Energy Strategy for British Columbia. 1994. Vancouver, British Columbia: British Columbia Energy Council.

BCH
Bringing Electricity to the Livable Region. 1994. Vancouver, British Columbia: BC Hydro

BCT
Transit and Land Use Planning. 1994. Surrey, British Columbia: BC Transit Long Range Planning.

CORE
Finding Common Ground: A Shared Vision For Land Use In British Columbia. 1994. Vancouver, British Columbia: Commission on Resources and Environment.

CS
City of Surrey Official Community Plan Background Report No. 1; Surrey: Existing Policies. 1994. Surrey, British Columbia: City of Surrey .

CV
Clouds of Change: Final Report of the City of Vancouver Task Force on Atmospheric Change. 1990. Vancouver, British Columbia: City of Vancouver.

LRS
Livable Region Strategy: Proposals. 1993. Burnaby, British Columbia: Greater Vancouver Regional District. (Also see *1995 Livable Region Strategic Plan*, Approved in Principle by the GVRD Board of Directors, Dec 9, 1994)

MA
Bill 11 – 1995, *Growth Strategies Statutes Amendment Act*, 1995. 1995. Victoria British Columbia: Province of British Columbia Legislative Assembly and Minister of Municipal Affairs. (see also: *Growth Strategies Statutes and Amendment Act: Explanatory Notes.* 1995. Victoria British Columbia: Province of British Columbia, Ministry of Municipal Affairs.)

THE DESIGN BRIEF

Introduction

This design brief should be the basis for your proposals. The charrette organizers have made every effort to ensure that the brief will promote comparability between the different teams without limiting your design discretion and expression.

You should assume that the plan you propose would take up to twenty years to carry out, and that during that time land ownership would naturally turn over to the land uses that you propose. You should assume that most existing site infrastructure (i.e. streets [except King George Highway] bridges, sewer lines, etc.) would need re-construction during this period, and could be realigned or reconfigured in conformance with your proposals.

Minimum and maximum population figures represent a range between high and very high when compared to the surrounding existing context.

The choice and relative proportion of dwelling types should be determined by each team. However, current market forces in Surrey strongly favour certain dwelling types over others (figures showing current City of Surrey market housing production by type are provided elsewhere in this binder). Some teams may conclude that achieving more sustainable sites and communities will require a radical departure from current market forces; these teams will favour a dwelling mix that the market does not presently support. Other teams may conclude that achieving more sustainable site and community design does not necessarily conflict with market forces. A list of common dwelling types and the land required for the different types is included in the appendix.

The site is ecologically sensitive. Protecting the site, its fish habitat values in particular, should be the highest priority. Based on the information provided, charrette participants should decide how best to protect and perhaps enhance the ecological func-tion of the site. Accommodating up to 15,000 people on the site may impinge on this imperative. You are asked to make your best judgement in the face of this conflict.

The commercial space requirements listed below represent a range between high and very high when compared to other new communities in our region. These numbers suggest that most of the residents in the communities you propose will make their major purchases in the community and/or that the community will attract customers from the surrounding areas.

Light industrial and office space requirements support the City of Surrey's desire to provide one job for every worker (18–65 years old) within Surrey. The target of providing job sites for one worker per household recognizes that many workers who live in the district will be employed elsewhere.

Finally and perhaps most importantly, the site is an element in the larger urban landscape – a cell in a larger cultural and bio-physical organism. The policies that inform the program for this site will guide urban development throughout the Province. Therefore, assume that adjacent sites would be compatible with your team's, and that eventually an urban pattern made up of many compatible sites would eventually result. Design teams should seek ways to include this larger context in their design process. Teams should also seek ways to express their idea of this larger context in their design proposal.

RESIDENTS

Total Site Area:	400 acres	160 hectares
Proposed Community Population[1]	Minimum 9,000	Maximum 15,000
Proposed Total Dwelling Units	Minimum 3,200	Maximum 5,400
Residential Parking Standard	1.25 spaces per dwelling unit – .25 spaces per elderly or special needs unit.[2] Parking can be on street or in surface lots.	
Gross Residential Density	Minimum 8 DU per acre, 20 DU per hectare	Maximum 14 DU per acre, 35 DU per hectare

OPEN SPACE[3]

	Minimum 60 acres (24 hectares) of unpaved public recreation and open space areas. Consideration of all environmentally sensitive lands for inclusion in open space system.	Maximum unlimited. Open space to include community and neighbourhood common spaces, playgrounds, parks, sports fields, conservation areas, community gardens, bicycle and walking networks, and other open, spaces.

PUBLIC TRANSIT

One or two light rail stops on King George Highway are anticipated. The exact locations of these stops have yet to be determined and should be suggested. Frequent bus connections from King George Highway to Surrey City Centre and the Sky Train station are presently available.[4]

COMMERCIAL

Commercial Space[5]	Minimum, 30,000 sq. ft. (2,800 sq. mtr.) per 1,000 population.	Maximum, 42,000 sq. ft. (3,900 sq. mtr.) per 1,000 population.
Commercial Parking Standard	750 sq. ft. or 70 sq. mtr. (3 spaces) per 1000 sq. ft. retail. On street and off street parking.[6]	

LIGHT INDUSTRIAL/OFFICE

Light Industrial/Corporate Office Space	25,000 sq. ft. (2,300 sq. mtr.) per 1,000 population.[7]
Service Office Space	16,000 sq. ft. (1,500 sq. mtr.) per 1,000 population.[8]
Light Industrial/Corporate Office/ Service Office Parking Standard	400 sq. ft. or 37 sq. mtr. (1.5 spaces) per 1,000 sq. ft. (or 90 sq. mtr.) office/light industrial.[9]

PUBLIC BUILDINGS

Elementary Schools

Two schools at 35,000 sq. ft. (or 3,200 sq. mtr.) each, for 500 students, access to 8 acres (3.25 hectares) of outdoor recreation space (outdoor recreation space can count toward minimum open space requirement). On street or off street parking for 25 cars.[10] Adequate middle and high school facilities exist within one mile of site.

Child Care Facilities and Preschools

2,560 sq. ft. (240 sq. mtr.) interior space, 4,800 sq. ft. (445 sq. mtr.) exterior play space per 1,000 dwelling units.[11]

Community Centre and Library

One at 36,000 sq. ft. (3,340 sq. mtr.) – on street or off street parking for 32 cars.

Fire Hall

One at 11,000 sq.. ft. (1,020 sq. mtr.).

Town Hall/Public Offices

20,000 sq. ft. (1,860 sq. mtr.) for city and provincial satellite health, records, social, job training and other public functions. On street or off street parking for 25 cars.

Churches/Multi Faith Centre with Assembly Hall

One per 4,000 population at 10,000 sq. ft. (930 sq. mtr.). On street or off street parking for 60 cars. Parking can be shared with non competing use.[12]

Notes

1
Minimum and maximum population, total dwelling units, and gross density figures are derived from a variety of sources that suggest eight dwelling units per acre is the minimum density at which a good range of commercial services can be economically provided. The higher figure is more in line with those who suggest that eight dwelling units per acre is still too low to sufficiently reduce energy and land consumption. Given the constraints imposed by the site, design teams must determine what population is appropriate for this site and how it should be deployed.

2
This number is one half the standard suburban residential parking requirement. One half standard is assumed to be appropriate for our purposes, given the "walking distance to services and transit" assumption underlying this charrette.

3
Minimum open space requirements are derived from current City of Surrey minimum standards, equivalent to minimum standards from Time Saver Standards for Site Planning. Breakdown is as follows: neighbourhood park, .6 ha per 1,000 pop; community park, .8 ha per 1,000 population; passive open space, .8 ha per 1,000 population. Maximum open space is unlimited. The proportion of the site that you decide to reserve as open space may be consequent to your assessment of the site's ecological sensitivity.

4
BC Transit intends to build a light rail line to connect South Newton to the Sky Train Station in Surrey City Centre. We anticipate that this rail line will be constructed at grade and be similar to the Portland, Oregon system. The rail line will be built within the existing King George Highway right of way. Minor changes to the rail line alignment may be proposed as part of your design proposal.

5
The minimum figure represents 70% of the 42,000 sq. ft. (3,900 sq. mtr.) per 1,000 persons commercial floor space ratio that exists in our region at this time. Since most new commercial space is now segregated into regional shopping centres, the amount of commercial space within walking distance of new dwellings is usually much lower than this figure. Given the "walking distance to services" and "access to transit" assumptions underlying this charrette, the 70% minimum figure was considered appropriate. The maximum figure represents 100 % of GVRD average for the region of 42,000 sq. ft. per 1,000 persons. Using the higher number suggests that all consumer needs can and should be met in the district.

6
This number is one half the standard suburban commercial requirement cited in Time Saver Standards for Site Planning. The UDI standard for retail parking is 5 to 6 spaces per 1000 sq. ft. (93 sq. mtr.) of commercial space. One half standard is assumed to be appropriate for our purposes, given the "walking distance to services and transit" assumption underlying this charrette.

7
This number is generated as follows: assume one job per household (UDI) and 2.87 persons per household. The number of jobs for the entire district should be 350 per 1,000 population. Assume 35% of jobs are in corporate office/light industrial. .35 X 350 = 123 jobs. 123 jobs x 200+ sq. ft. (19 sq. mtr.) per worker = 25,000 ft. (2,300 sq. mtr.) per 1,000 population.

8
23% of 350 workers per 1,000 population = 80 persons at 200+ sq. ft. (19 sq. mtr.) per person = 16,000 sq. ft. (1,500 sq. mtr.) per 1,000 population.

9
This number is one half the standard suburban light industrial/corporate office parking space requirement cited in Time Saver Standards for Site Planning. The UDI standard is 3.5 spaces per 1,000 sq. ft. of office. One half this standard is assumed appropriate for our purposes given the "walking distance to jobs or transit" assumption underlying this charrette.

10
Source, City of Surrey Schools.

11
Source, City of Surrey Planning Dept.

12
This number is an estimate of the typical number of churches per 1,000 population in our region, including all denominations.

DESIGN CHARRETTE
ADVISORY BOARD

James Taylor Chair in Landscape
and Liveable Environments

The following individuals kindly agreed to serve as members of the Sustainable Urban Landscapes Advisory Board. This group met at key points to advise on all aspects of the project plan, to select the case study site, to review and amend the design program, and to advise the Chair on appropriate follow up activities subsequent to the charrette event.

Mr. Michael Geller
Principal
The Geller Group
601 West Cordova
Vancouver, BC, V6B 1G1

Penelope Gurstein
Assistant Professor
UBC School of Community and Regional
Planning
6333 Memorial Road
Vancouver, BC, V6T 1Z2

Sanford Hirshen
Director and Professor
UBC School of Architecture
6333 Memorial Road
Vancouver, BC, V6T 1Z2

Mr. Burton Leon
Manager of Policy and Long Range
Planning
Planning and Development Department,
City of Surrey
14245 - 56th Avenue
Surrey, BC, V3X 3A2
Tel: 591-4282 Fax: 591-2507

Mr. Erik Karlsen
Director, Special Projects
B.C. Ministry of Municipal Affairs
4th Floor, 800 Johnson Street
Victoria, BC, V7V 1X4

Mr. Hugh Kellas
Administrator, Policy Development
Strategic Planning Dept.
Greater Vancouver Regional District
4330 Kingsway
Burnaby, BC, V5H 4G8

Mr. Dale McClanaghan
President and CEO
Van City Enterprises Ltd.
4th Floor-515 West 10th Avenue
Vancouver, BC V5Z 4A8

Ms. Stacy Moriarty
Principal, Moriarty/Condon
Landscape Architects Ltd.
Suite 102 - 1661 West 2nd Avenue
Vancouver, B.C. V6J 1H3

Patrick Mooney
Associate Professor
UBC Landscape Architecture Program
Suite 248 - 2357 Main Mall
Vancouver B.C. V6T 1Z4

Mr. Kelvin Neufeld
Member, Legislative and Public Affairs
Committee
Fraser Valley Real Estate Board
Box 99, Surrey, BC

John Robinson
Director, UBC Sustainable Development
Research Institute
Professor, UBC School of Geography
B5 2202 Main Mall
Vancouver, BC, V6T 1Z4
Tel: 822-8198 Fax: 822-9191

Ms. Elizabeth Watts
Coordinator, Sustainable Urban Landscapes
Design Charrette
UBC Landscape Architecture Program
Suite 248 - 2357 Main Mall
Vancouver B.C. V6T 1Z4

DESIGN CHARRETTE
TEAM LEADERS

Joost Bakker, Architect

Joost Bakker is a partner in Hotson Bakker Architects, with offices in Toronto and Vancouver Canada. The firm has received international recognition for such projects as the redevelopment of Granville Island in Vancouver and the Sanctuary Cove Resort in Queensland, Australia. He is a past member of the Vancouver Planning Commission and the Vancouver Heritage Commission. He worked with Professor Quayle on the award wining Greenways, Public Ways Report and is actively involved in the thesis program at the School of Architecture at the University of British Columbia.

Cheryl Barton, Landscape Architect

Cheryl Barton is the principal of The Office of Cheryl Barton in San Francisco, California. Her work has been recognized with many awards including the ASLA Honour Award for the Sutro Historic District in 1993. Her design work and writings have been published in many North American design magazines and journals. Barton is a Fellow and Past President of the American Society of Landscape Architects.

Catherine Brown, Landscape Architect

Catherine Brown is Coordinator of Special Projects and the Dayton Hudson Senior Fellow in Urban Design for the Design Center for American Urban Landscape at the University of Minnesota. Brown was a founding principal of the design firm CITY-WEST, who, in this capacity, directed a broad range of progressive urban design projects throughout the U.S.

Patrick Condon, Landscape Architect

Professor Condon currently holds the UBC Chair in Landscapes and Liveable Environments at the University of British Columbia. From 1981 to 1983 he was the Director of Community Development for the City of Westfield, Massachusetts and from 1984-1991 he taught landscape architecture at

the University of Minnesota. He has won awards for his teaching and research and has published and lectured widely on sustainable urban design and landscape design theory.

Roger Hughes, Architect

Roger Hughes is an architect currently living and working in Vancouver, BC. His firm, Roger Hughes Architects, works on various institutional and residential projects. While working in London England he gained experience in the restoration of historic buildings for re-use as housing. His work has been recognized nationally by many awards programs. Sustainable high density housing is one of Roger's special areas of expertise. Mr. Hughes frequently serves the School of Architecture at the University of British Columbia as an invited critic.

Ken Greenberg, Architect

Ken Greenberg is a partner with the Toronto firm Berridge Lewinberg Greenberg Dark Gabor where he specializes in the rejuvenation and intensification of inner city areas and the creation of denser mixed use communities on the urban fringe. Along with many international involvements, Greenberg is currently preparing a Development Framework for the Capitol City river-front along the Mississippi in St. Paul, Minnesota. He has taught and lectured widely in North America and Europe and has contributed to many professional journal, books, and publications in the field of urban design.

Doug Kelbaugh, Architect

Doug Kelbaugh is Professor of Architecture and Urban Design at the University of Washington and principal in Kelbaugh & Associates in Seattle, Washington. His designs have been published in over 100 books and magazines and featured in many exhibitions world wide. Professor Kelbaugh has taught and lectured at many schools of architecture throughout the US and

Europe. He co-edited *The Pedestrian Pocket Book*, co-chaired four national and international conferences on energy and design, organized over a dozen national and international design charrettes and consulted on private and public development projects locally and abroad.

Jennifer Marshall, Architect
Jennifer Marshall is a principal in Marshall Fisher Architects. She is actively involved in architectural education and has been teaching design studio at UBC since 1988. Her chief interests lie in the areas of urban design, housing, and architectural ideas. She has won many awards during her career, particularly for her sensitive architectural restorations.

Stacy Moriarty, Landscape Architect
Stacy Moriarty is president of Moriarty/ Condon Landscape Architects and Planners Ltd, in Vancouver, BC. She has an international practice, with project experience across the United States and in British Columbia. Ms. Moriarty has won many awards including the Rome Prize in Landscape Architecture from the American Academy in Rome. Her writings, drawings and projects have been featured in numerous exhibitions and articles in North America and abroad.

William Morrish, Architect
William Morrish, director of the Design Center for American Urban Landscape, holds the Dayton Hudson land grant chair in urban design in the College of Architecture and Landscape Architecture at the University of Minnesota. He has taught, lectured and published extensively in the fields of architecture, urban design, and related topics. As well, he was a co-founder of the urban design firm CITYWEST.

Moura Quayle, Landscape Architect
Moura Quayle is a Professor in the Landscape Architecture Program at the University of British Columbia. She is actively committed to urban landscape advocacy work by lobbying for greenway programs and residential street renovations. Her involvement in City of Vancouver's Urban Landscape Task Force has won her many awards locally and internationally.

Murray Silverstein, Architect
Murray Silverstein is a founding partner in Jacobson Silverstein Winslow Architects in Berkeley, California, where his work in and around the San Francisco Bay Area has won a number of awards. In addition to his work as practitioner, he has authored and co-authored books and articles including *A Pattern Language*, which has gained world-wide recognition. Silverstein has also taught and lectured in architecture at a number of Universities throughout the U.S.

Ron Walkey, Architect
Ron Walkey is an Associate Professor in the UBC School of Architecture. He has expressed his passion for building and for cities in many important pilot projects such as the False Creek South district in Vancouver. In this project, and in the important Britannia Services Centre project, also in Vancouver, Professor Walkey conclusively demonstrated the value of *Pattern Language* (Alexander et. al.) to the design process. Professor Walkey has published widely, most recently in *Dwelling, Seeing. and Designing: Toward a Phenomenological Ecology.* Edited by David Seamon. 1993. Albany N.Y.: S.U.N.Y. Press

Bill Wenk, Landscape Architect
Bill Wenk is president of Wenk Associates Inc., a planning and landscape architecture firm based in Denver, Colorado. He is a member of the American Society of Landscape Architects, and is a member of the Conservation Funds National Forum on Non-point Source Water Pollution. His firm's work along urban rivers and streams has been recognized nationally and internationally for its environmental responsibility, and for the integration of urban and natural systems.

Carolyn Woodland, Landscape Architect
Carolyn Woodland is president of Hough Woodland Naylor Dance Limited, a Toronto based environmental planning and design firm. She also teaches landscape architecture at the University of Toronto, and contributes to many publications and articles on topics of ecological design, open space planning and waterfront development. Her environmental urban site planning projects have won numerous awards and attracted international attention. She is a co-author of *Restoring Natural Habitats*, published in association with Toronto's Waterfront Regeneration Trust.

Don Wuori, Landscape Architect
Don Wuori is a principal in the firm Philips Wuori Long Inc. in Vancouver, BC. The firm's work focuses on the planning, design and implementation of waterfront public parks, and open space, urban design, public art, and mixed use developments. His award winning projects have been recognized by organizations locally as well as nationally.